THE CASE OF WALTER BAGEHOT

THE CASE
of
WALTER BAGEHOT

C. H. Sisson

FABER AND FABER
LONDON

First edition 1972
Published by
Faber and Faber Limited
3 Queen Square, London WC1

Printed in Great Britain by
Western Printing Services Ltd
Bristol

ISBN 0571 09501 1

*Any old lie to cheat England out of the best
so that the tenth best may have a chance.*

E. Gordon Craig

O, das grässliche Lachen des Golds.

Georg Trakl

CONTENTS

CONTENTS

AUTHOR'S NOTE

Nearly a hundred years after his death–which was in 1877–the writings of Walter Bagehot are still in lively circulation. There is scarcely any other Victorian journalism of which the same can be said. Bagehot was successful in getting a hearing in his own time, and he is now selling well in paper-back here and in the United States. There have been numerous editions of his main works, and they have been extensively read, for more than a century, both by students and by people actively concerned with public affairs. A definitive edition of his *Collected Works* is in process of publication by *The Economist*, of which journal he was one of the early editors.

So wide and enduring a success is sufficient proof that Bagehot was saying something which successive generations thought was important and wanted to hear. What, in brief, was this? The works are remarkably diverse in subject matter. Bagehot wrote on a variety of literary subjects; on the English Constitution; on the money-market; as an eye-witness in Paris, on Louis Napoleon's *coup* of 1851; as editor of *The Economist* from 1861, on a multitude of domestic and foreign affairs. The work would not hold together at all but for a thread running through the whole. What is the nature of this thread? In all his studies Bagehot hankered after 'the living reality' and distrusted 'the paper description'. So do we. Was his method of arriving at his wholly laudable objective a valid one? Is his scalpel useful for our own enquiries?

There are in all three collected editions of Bagehot's works, including the one still in course of issue. The first was published in 1889 by the Traveller's Insurance Company of Hartford, Connecticut–a mysterious departure from that institution's ordinary line of business. The current *Economist* edition was commissioned by Sir Geoffrey Crowther in 1959 and is being edited by Mr. St. John Stevas. The first two volumes, containing the *Literary Essays*, appeared in 1965. Two volumes of *Historical Essays* followed in 1968 and a further five volumes are planned. In between these two editions came an edition edited by Bagehot's sister-in-law, Mrs. Russell Barrington, and published by Longmans, Green & Co. in 1915. This contains some matter not in the insurance company's edition; the *Economist* edition will contain much further new material, most of it from that periodical. Even Mr. St. John Stevas does not, mercifully, aim at including every word that Bagehot ever wrote. All three editions contain all of Bagehot's principal works and for the ordinary reader those, and some sampling of the occasional articles, will be enough.

In this essay I have throughout given detailed references to the 1915 edition which, pending the completion of Mr. St. John Stevas's project, gives the best general view of Bagehot's work. Where the reference is to material included in one of the volumes of the *Economist* edition which has already appeared, I have supplemented it by indicating, on the first occasion when a particular article is mentioned, where it is to be found in those volumes. Thus a footnote which reads '*Works*, I, p. 77 (*E*. IV, 29)' means that the quotation is to be found on p. 77 of volume I of the 1915 edition and that the article from which it is taken is also to be found on p. 29 of volume IV of the *Economist* edition. Later footnotes referring to the same article will give only references to the 1915 edition.

The 1915 edition is in ten volumes, the tenth containing Mrs. Barrington's *Life* of her brother-in-law. This tenth volume is referred to in footnotes as Barrington, *Life*, followed by the page reference.

CHAPTER ONE

How Walter Bagehot was Made

It does not do to make too much of a man's birth-place. It is not necessary, perhaps, to have a picture of the two hills, which fixed Langport at a crossing of the River Parrett, or of the easily-flooded moors at their feet, to understand Bagehot's orientation as he set out. It may not matter whether the Belgae were once encamped, as the historian of the town asserts, on the side of the river which has long carried the main population, while the Damnonii watched them from Herd's Hill, on the other side—the hill now topped by the house Bagehot's grandfather built and which was his parents' home and his own after he was ten years old. But it is of interest that the town was twice touched by war in the seventeenth century, once in 1645 when Cromwell pursued Goring through the burning streets, and again in 1685, when Monmouth was defeated only a few miles away, on Sedgemoor. It was from the trading and industrial towns of that part of Somerset that Monmouth recruited the unfortunates who were cut up in the ditches around Westonzoyland. The Langport of 1826, when Bagehot was born, was still a significant centre of local trade. Throughout the eighteenth century the Parrett had carried corn, stone, brick, tiles, timber, coal, iron and salt. Vessels went to and from all coasting ports, according to the *British Directory* for 1780, and 'the Taunton Waggon' dropped goods from London 'to be carried further by water'. With all this trade the families of both Bagehot's father and his mother were extensively connected. Stuckeys and Bagehots had wharves and warehouses at Langport many years before Walter was born; indeed they had long dominated the town. It was a place of waggons and barges, and out of this freight trade the banking business, on which the author of *Lombard Street* floated into the world, sprang. It was in the old Bank House, in the main street of Langport, that Walter Bagehot was born. As late as 1866 the firm of Stuckey and Bagehot had a lot of money in shipping, owning twenty-four East Indiamen as well as barges on the local river.

It was on the side of Walter's mother that the commercial genius of these dynasties was most vividly exhibited. Her brother Vincent Stuckey, who kept court at Hill House, on the site of what had formerly been the Bagehot residence, was characterised by a good fortune which he seems never to have been backward in seconding. As a young man he presented himself before Lady Chatham, at Burton Pynsent, which is only a few miles from Langport, and asked her to give him an introduction to the Prime Minister, her son. The very words of her reply, 'Well, I do not see why I should not', seem to have been treasured in the Stuckey family, as well they might be. Vincent took Lady Chatham's letter to London, where he no doubt presented it with any necessary effrontery. He was not born to fail. He obtained a clerkship in the Treasury, and was for a time private secretary to Pitt, also to Huskisson. He seems to have retained his political and other London friends when, after a few years, he went back to pursue his own business interests in the west country. His uncle Samuel Stuckey, who died in 1812, was already doing quite a lot of banking privately. Vincent was, however, enabled to establish his famous firm partly by another piece of good fortune to which his own enterprise contributed. On holiday in Devon, while still employed at the Treasury, he looked up an old bachelor squire to tell him he had the privilege of having the same surname. Squire Stuckey was so flattered by this attention that, when he died, he left Vincent a life interest in his estates in Devon and at Compton and South Petherton. Vincent must have been intended by heaven to be a banker.

Walter's father, Thomas Watson Bagehot, who when Walter was born and for long afterwards managed the Langport branch of the family bank, seems to have depended on the common qualities of earnestness and ordinary diligence. Walter's biographer, his sister-in-law Mrs. Russell Barrington, whose comments reflect charmingly the social tone of the *milieu*, says: 'As a family the Bagehots were more intellectual than the Stuckeys. They were less robust, more retiring and dignified—perhaps more highly cultured.' And one wonders what faint chill in the Langport relationships is indicated by the further comment: 'The Bagehot family influenced the people of Langport by personal dignity and refinement, which qualities, though probably hardly recognised by the county folk for what they were, gave weight to their position.'[1] The family was certainly outside the system of society which then so firmly—if less firmly in Somerset than in Gloucestershire or Wiltshire—prevailed in farming and land-owning England. The Stuckeys and the Bagehots were, so to speak, the great senatorial families of this tiny borough, with its two main streets, its river, its Portreeve and corporation. Bagehot must have grown up in an atmosphere of Venetian democracy, in which it was silently asserted that no one outside had a right to look down on the great trading families and that no one in Langport had a right not to look up to them. Vincent Stuckey, with an eye to the main chance, was at the time of Bagehot's birth 'going about amongst the country families, persuading them to close the small country banks and invest in his, when he would find appointments for their sons in the branches of Stuckey.'[2] Thomas Bagehot, 'more intellectual', had to establish some consonance between his ideas and his aspirations, and had become a Unitarian, so reverting to a vein which had appeared in an earlier generation of his family. He had 'a quiet obstinate tenacity', says Mrs. Barrington, and in view of the genteel moderation of her expression, and her nearness to him, one can give credence to that. He was of course 'a decided Whig, but he took an intellectual rather than a party view of politics'.[3] It is of course not party politics to agree with a Whig, only to disagree with him. For all

[1] Barrington, *Life*, pp. 60–1.   [3] Barrington, *Life*, p. 61.
[2] D. M. Ross, *Langport and its Church*, Herald Press, Langport, 1911, p. 358.

his geniality and adaptability – a Stuckey inheritance – Walter was evidently a chip off the old block.

With Walter's mother the affinities were more delicate. She was a Stuckey, and therefore not an intellectual. 'Not an intellectual woman', reaffirms Norman St. John Stevas 'and consequently had strong opinions on most matters.'[1] She did not become a Unitarian nor, it may be added, a Papist, following that other drift of the times. She remained an Anglican, as befitted someone not given to thought. All agree she was gay, lively, perhaps a trifle bustling. For Mrs. Barrington she had 'intellectual vivacity', which is not incompatible with the omission of certain forms of thought. There was an underlay of weakness below the activity of the Stuckeys, who were not necessarily the worse for that. If Edith Bagehot had to keep going, like her brother Vincent, it was perhaps because of a fear which, in her, became patent in fits of madness. This was the skeleton in Bagehot's domestic cupboard, and the matter can never have been far from his thoughts. He seems throughout his life to have been beyond reproach in the care and sympathy he showed for his mother's difficulties. It is no small counterpoise to the notion one has of the active, power-loving, clever man of the world, for ever taking trains and writing articles. The menace of insanity had been reinforced by the presence, when Walter was a boy at home, of Vincent Estlin, his mother's child by her first marriage, who was in some way permanently deranged. Walter must have thought of these things when he was contemplating his own marriage with Eliza Wilson. They never had any children.

With a man whose work bears, as clearly as Bagehot's does, the imprint of his beginnings, it is naturally of interest to ask what

[1] Norman St. John Stevas, *Walter Bagehot, A Study of his life and thought together with a selection from his political writings*, Eyre & Spottiswoode, London, 1959, p. 2.

he was taught by way of religion and how far he re-made his thought in later years. This is not to broach the question so boldly settled by St. John Stevas with the words 'Walter Bagehot was a deeply religious man'.[1] But there are intellectual forms which can be traced, and it was certainly significant for Bagehot's development that, every Sunday morning, he attended, in the drawing-room of his home, a Unitarian service at which his father presided, while in the afternoon he went with his mother to the parish church. This oscillation helped him to grow up cautiously. It was perhaps out of politeness to his mother, or some more tender concern, that led him to incline, in a rather elusive way, to her side of the argument. Thomas Bagehot, preaching and praying on the top of the hill where the church wasn't, must have left a profound impression. The social implications of this divisive activity are not to be ignored. The bank-manager and merchant, who all the week dominated the affairs of Langport from the Bank House in the main street, reappeared in a dominant position each Sunday in the mansion on the hill of the Damnonii to which, on the death of Walter's grandfather, he had withdrawn or promoted the family. As a mere dumb-show, without considering a word that may have been said, it is a masque of Protestant dissent. There seems to be little information as to who was in Thomas's congregation. It would be interesting to know. Those who were there laid under tribute were perhaps not those who found it easiest to get an overdraft from the Bank House. No doubt Walter, looking back, would find his father's Sunday morning too overt a manifestation of reason and trade for his religious assent to settle there. The compromises and evasions of the Prayer Book would perhaps have suited him better, even if he had not been bound, as a politically-minded man, to recognise the social viability of the Established Church. What kind of thoughts Walter Bagehot had about religion is obscure. One has to reckon with the fact that, in his life-time, much discourse which would now run into other channels was then conducted in

[1] St. John Stevas, *op. cit.*, p. 25.

near-theological terms. There is a characteristic passage on his approach to theology in one of the letters written to Eliza Wilson during their courtship. After admitting 'I still like to talk theology very much when I am started'—and perhaps the 'still' suggests that he was moving away from that disposition and the 'like to talk . . . very much' suggests an element of sporting conversationalism—he goes on:

'I am afraid however you give me credit for more digested and elaborate ideas on the subject than I really have. The faith of young men is rather *tentative*. Some points of course are very fixed, but a good many are wavering, are rather tendencies than conclusions. I have perhaps an unusual degree of this myself. From my father and mother being of different—I am afraid I might say—*opposite* sentiments on many points, I was never taught any scheme of doctrine as an absolute certainty in the way most people are. What I have made out is a good deal my own doing, and naturally it seems to require testing more than an hereditary belief would. I have always had an indistinct feeling that my inner life has been too harsh and vacant to give me an abiding hold of some parts of religion. At any rate the outline wants deepening and the colours softening. You never know the intellectual consequences of a new moral experience. It is a new premiss and may combine with any one of your previous results. Women arrive more easily at their conclusions on these subjects because their spiritual experience is gentler and more continuous, less of a seizure in fact, as I said just now. They are often therefore puzzled at the way men go to and fro, apparently settling a conclusion today and unsettling it tomorrow, and think it is aimless wandering and that nothing is being gained. But it is not so. A new spiritual consciousness naturally recalls the mind to consideration; and if sometimes it brings us back to old opinions and teaches us that our *last* opinions are not so well-founded as we thought them, yet the "old" opinion is really a new one because based on and cleared up by a new spirit, perhaps from God, and it is necessary for thinking men at each stage to think out the *data* they have, though they know those data may change tomorrow. If they did not do so, they would not know how to appreciate each change or be sure of its effects – the mind would become confusion.'[1]

The passage marks clearly enough the effect on Bagehot's mind of the domestic opposition he was brought up among. It is also notable as the apologia of a man of the world, in a time and circle in which it was taken for granted that a man had a religion, to a girl he was undoubtedly very anxious to please. Bagehot cannot fail to present himself as the bustling, independent young man who has charmed the Wilson sisters. The scheme of doctrine he has worked out – and which he avoids indicating–is, he says, 'a good deal my own doing', an expression which no doubt came readily from his practical, do-it-yourself mind but is odd in relation to the subject-matter. He has no hereditary belief, he in effect says, as many a young man might without having behind him the peculiar divisions of Bagehot's childhood. The theory that his 'inner life has been too harsh and vacant' for 'an abiding hold on some parts of religion' is more profoundly characteristic. For it suggests–in spite of all that follows about the founding opinions on facts–that not truth but a suitable frame of mind is what is in question. Women–in the more fortunate classes, he must have meant–have that frame of mind more easily because their life is gentler. There is a touch of Victorian domestic comedy about this.

Whether Bagehot's theology followed more closely his father's or his mother's side, there is no question which had the determining effect on his education. An old acquaintance describes Thomas Bagehot as 'remarkably plodding,'[2] and one imagines that while the Stuckey fireworks went off around him he advanced to his modest objectives with some assurance. It would be wrong to represent the Unitarianism to which Bagehot was thus early

[1] *The Love-Letters of Walter Bagehot and Eliza Wilson*, Faber, London, 1933, pp. 82–3.
[2] Barrington, *Life*, p. 63. The old acquaintance was Henry Sawtell, a distant cousin of the Stuckeys.

introduced as a mere whim of his father's or merely as a recurrent freak in the Bagehot line. Walter Bagehot was born in a period which saw, at the same time as the Oxford movement, another thrust of the Protestantism which, ever since the Reformation—and it may be said, for some time before that event was officially billed—has penetrated ever more deeply into the popular mind, and of which the most extreme form, whatever that might currently be, has long seemed the 'natural' form of thought for people in an age of science and industry. One can think of Cudworth and Whichcote as among the progenitors of the more rational side of this movement. It was anyhow from such Christian, rather than from Deist sources, that what came to be called Unitarianism took its colour. It was earnest and Puritan and, as it were, never quite realised how much it had thrown away in its passion for reason and dissent. The west country had had its share of this movement, with the trading towns of course in the lead.

Thomas Bagehot watched his son's education with vicarious ambition. 'Every day,' he wrote to him when the boy was sixteen, 'do I feel how much I have lost in not having had such an education as I wish to give you, and you need not therefore fear that anything will be wanting on my part to secure to you its advantages. I do not repine although I feel that there is a world beyond my ken, and that that world of knowledge and usefulness may bring with it more happiness than can be mine.'[1] It was a kind of repining, however, and to a boy of sixteen perhaps a little oppressive. There was a trace of romantic disappointment about Thomas Bagehot, and one senses that he consoled himself in the gloom of the Bank House by the hope that it was only his circumstances which made him the mediocrity that he was. Walter

[1] Barrington, *Life*, p. 97.

Bagehot was first put into the hands of a governess, and shortly afterwards sent to the Langport Grammar School, where he remained up to the age of twelve. The school was an old one, re-constituted after the Restoration but evidently of much earlier origin. The Corporation had an interest in it and the boys were expected to be in their place in the parish church on Sundays. Whether or not it was in this connection that Walter Bagehot became acquainted with Secker on the Catechism—an acquaintance so early and impressive that he said in his essay on Bishop Butler, written in 1854, that 'the name of the writer is now with some so associated by early habit that it is difficult to fancy even Butler on equal social terms with him'[1]—there is no doubt that he received a solid Anglican instruction to set off against his father's heresies. The school had for a long time been housed in the hanging chapel, over the old east gate of the town and hard by the church, but by Bagehot's day it had moved nearer the Bank House. Stuckeys and Bagehots were of course among the trustees, who seem to have decided, individually or collectively, what pupils should be admitted. Shortly before Walter Bagehot started to attend there was a social change, not necessarily for the better, in the character of the Grammar School—a limitation in the number of free places, 'the National School henceforth providing for the children of the poor'.[2] The master remained the same, however. He was one W. Quekett, who had been in post since 1790. He seems to have been a schoolmaster of some gifts, and altogether served there for more than fifty years. The small grammar schools of this epoch must have been of an individuality unimaginable in our own time, sometimes very bad, no doubt, but sometimes extremely good. One thinks of William Barnes's schools in Mere and Dorchester. Walter Bagehot was not without fellow-pupils of intelligence and social standing. Two of them became generals and one a Premier of New Zealand, which might at least be evidence that the bank manager's son was not left to lord it alone in the school. He was, however, destined for a more

---

[1] *Works*, I, p. 269 (*E*, I, 217).   [2] Ross, *op. cit.*, p. 332.

sophisticated education. The next step was to Bristol College, a school which has not survived but seems to have been among the more enterprising of its day. Walter had a more individual advantage during his stay in Bristol. His mother's brother-in-law, Dr. Prichard, who lived there, was a noted ethnologist, and Walter thus had access to scientific circles in Clifton and seems to have circulated in them to his profit, meeting conversation on such subjects as 'the Arrow-headed character and the monuments of Peutapolis, and the way of manufacturing cloth in the South Seas.'[1] Dr. Prichard was the subject of a memoir by John Addington Symonds, a member of the Bristol circle and the father of the writer of the same name. Symonds lists Prichard's works as including *Researches into the Physical History of Mankind*–for which he was best known–*The Natural History of Man, Egyptian Mythology, The Eastern Origin of the Celtic Nations* and *The Review of the Doctrine of a Vital Principle*–this last apparently a tract against Priestley. Perhaps there was a little jealousy, and a little resentment against his wife's brilliant relations, in Thomas Bagehot's aspiration for his son's education and his expression of his own enforced contentment with the station in life to which he had been called. However that may be, there is no doubt that Bagehot had a fortunate boyhood. He was by nature capable of a wide range of intellectual interests, and his circumstances were such as to give him the right exercise early.

The question then was as to where he should pursue his university studies. No doubt Thomas Bagehot, as strategic overseer of his son's studies, had long pondered this subject and reached the foregone conclusion. It is echoed in an essay Walter Bagehot wrote at the age of sixteen, when the question was actual. Even a clever boy of sixteen rarely has thoughts which could properly be called his own, on other than personal subjects. Bagehot wrote that 'the recent formation of a new University conducted on less exclusive principles and a more extended plan than Oxford and Cambridge, will oblige these venerable insti-

---

[1] From a letter to his mother, quoted in Barrington, *Life*, p. 98.

tutions to include in their course of Study, subjects now beyond its limits, and to give up enough of their time-hallowed but now obsolete customs, to enable them to keep up with the Spirit of the age.'[1] The real reason for the choice of University College, London, was, of course, that Thomas Bagehot would not let his son subscribe formally to the Thirty-nine Articles. It would have been carrying liberalism too far to allow this victory to the religion of the Stuckeys, which was supposed also, though a little ambiguously, to be Walter's own. It is uncertain how far this choice of university seemed to Bagehot, in the long run, to have been the right one. No doubt in the end he ceased to think about the matter, and it suited well enough what was to be his rôle as the independent spirit with a bank balance, even a bank, of his own. But there can be no doubt that, at a certain depth, the exclusion rankled. The essay on Oxford, written when Bagehot was twenty-six, is full of the subject: 'here are, we will say, perhaps a hundred English youths, as clever, as able, as intellectual, as likely to participate in the full benefits of University instructions, as any other youths. Why then should they be excluded?'[2] The *onus probandi* was on the side of those who persisted in keeping out the élite to which Bagehot belonged or, truth to tell, half belonged. There follows an argument based on a rather untheological notion of the Church of England, which has been repeated since, in one form and another, by all kinds of liberals and dissenters, to the great delectation of Papists, to whose armoury it really belongs. This is that the Founders' wills were—most of them—made before the Church was reformed, and that therefore Post-Tridentine Papists should have preference over Anglicans. Bagehot does not put it quite like that. With heavy irony, 'it is . . . singular', he says, that the Founder 'should have always expressed a strong preference for the religion of others. No doubt it is so, if the augurs say so; but it is not quite what we should expect.'[3] With a snigger the whole claim of the Church of England to be the Catholic Church in this island is set aside—a motion which is

---

[1] *Works*, VIII, p. 233.   [2] *Works*, I, p. 175.   [3] *Works*, I, p. 176.

hardly excusable, in an educated Anglican, in 1852. Bagehot must have known what he was doing or, alternatively, have been carried away by personal *pique*. He was certainly not uninstructed. 'Theology never took a more prominent part in any layman's life of thought than it did in that of Walter Bagehot,'[1] says his biographer. And elsewhere: 'While studying law in London, Walter Bagehot paid various visits to Oxford'—about 1848—'staying with his friend Constantine Prichard, a fellow of Balliol. There he came under the influence of John Henry Newman, whose Anglican sermons he admired enormously.'[2] One sometimes gets the impression that Bagehot was an Anglican for the ladies. He might well maintain the appearance of this position for the benefit of his mother, for whose instability he always showed a laudable care, and no doubt his sister-in-law and future biographer, who was often about at Herd's Hill, would be presented with a similar front. 'English Dissent is a congeries of sects,' he says; 'the English Church is a congeries of sects.'[3] The equation could not be more complete. Bagehot comes very near to saying that the Church is an opinion, and this, perhaps, is what he thought it was.

The personal note in the essay on Oxford is intriguing. At one point we even get: 'A Unitarian marries a wife, and turns banker; his son is made a lord, and turns to the Church.'[4] There is no doubt about Bagehot's social obsessions. He was a climber, like his uncle Vincent Stuckey who asked to be introduced to the Prime Minister. He is strong in his sense of the Church of England as 'the religion of the wealthy', as if a poor banker was not rich enough to be admitted. If Oxford were opened to dissenters 'not an enormous number would go. It must be remembered that the theological division of the English people corresponds, though very roughly, with a social division. Nonconformists differ much from Conformists; their habits are different; their manners are different.'[5] Then he reverts to University College, London. 'All

[1] Barrington, *Life*, p. 80.   [2] Barrington, *Life*, p. 79.
[3] *Works*, I, p. 177.   [4] *Works*, I, p. 177.
[5] *Works*, I, p. 177.

this'—the social differences and so on—'was quite forgotten at the establishment of the London University. Lord Brougham is accustomed to describe the expectations of thronged halls, and eager students, and intense and ceaseless study; and the astonishment of the promoters at the moderate number, and calm demeanour and brief sojourn of those who responded to their call. Nor is the case altered now.' He goes on prophetically—but with a false prophecy: 'The expanse of Gower Street will not emulate the slopes of St. Geneviève. . . . The number of Nonconformists who desire to give their sons what can, in the English use of the term, be called a University education, is not very considerable, nor, according to the better authorities, does it increase. They do not design their sons in general for an intellectual life, for the learned professions, for business on a large scale or of a varied kind; they do not wish their sons to form aristocratic connections; but to be solicitors, attorneys, merchants, in a patient and useful way.' He rubbed it in. 'For this they think—and most likely they think rightly—that twenty years of life are quite an adequate preparation; they believe that more would in most cases interfere with the practised sagacity, the moderate habits, the simple wants, the routine inclinations, which are essential to the humbler sorts of practical occupation.' All this is rather astonishing, considering Bagehot's own background. But he always saw himself as a *homme d'élite*; what went for him did not go for other people. He went on to a further prophecy, again showing no great foresight, for a man who was to set the tone of political criticism for so many years. 'Open therefore the older Universities though you may, you will not practically increase or materially change the class who will resort to them; the Dissenters in Oxford will ever be a small, a feeble, an immaterial, though certainly a respectable and perhaps an erudite minority.'[1]

In the face of all this it is difficult to believe that the brave sentiments of the essay Bagehot wrote at sixteen really represent what he felt at being excluded from Oxford. The essay ten years

[1] *Works*, I, p. 178.

later is of interest also as illustrating his attitude to the Papists. St. John Stevas assures us that Bagehot 'always had an affection for the Roman Catholic Church, and accurately appreciated the true nature of Catholicism.'[1] What Bagehot said about the admission of its adherents to Oxford was that 'a Catholic Hall, we can believe, would really be a nuisance.' He was for admitting them all the same. 'The English leanings and prejudices,' he explained, 'are so contrary to Romanism, that it is only the semblance of persecution and the fortuitous opportunities of recent years which have occasioned its recent prominence.' This again shows little sense of the future. 'Familiarity will spoil romance'—such was his reasoning—'the charm of Romanism is its mystery.'[2] He might as truly have added that part of the attraction of English Romanism is in its dissenting spirit, in that it shares with Unitarianism, in this country, the charm of being against the established authorities.

Thomas Bagehot took his son to London in October, 1842 and delivered him into the hands of the Unitarian Dr. Hoppus, who kept a house for young men attending University College. Clearly it was intended that the boy's education should be conducted under the right auspices. Bagehot had hardly been there a month when a curious episode took place, which is not fully explained by his biographer and the full significance of which one therefore cannot judge. It is worth mentioning, however, because it indicates that, whatever the general state of Bagehot's beliefs at this time, he had no scepticism which extended to the ordinary rules of conduct. He reported two of his fellow-boarders to Dr. Hoppus. 'I feel,' he wrote to his father, 'that it cannot be my duty to allow this state of things to continue.'[3] What the two young men were up to is not clear, but it must have been one of the classic faults, for the revelation was followed by 'shock' on the part of Dr. Hoppus, a sending for the chief culprit's father, 'who seemed at first to be inclined to be very angry'—the implication is,

---

[1] St. John Stevas, *op. cit.*, p. 29.   [2] *Works*, I, pp. 178–9.
[3] Barrington, *Life*, p. 102.

with Bagehot as much as with his own son. Bagehot expressed to the bank manager his conviction that it was 'essential' to the culprit's welfare 'that he should be immediately removed from London.' This suggests that the temptations of the capital had been too much for the culprit. One cannot but think that the sixteen-year-old moralist was taking a bit much on himself. He was, perhaps, as in his essay on the advantages of University College, merely the medium of his father's sentiments. This episode was, however, evidently a moral crisis for Bagehot, though in true Puritan form one in which the morality of other people's conduct was at least as much in question as that of his own.

Thomas Bagehot's plans for his son worked out well, for he made friends of the right kind. In particular he became intimate with Richard Hutton, over-scrupulous, over-conscientious and of course Unitarian. It is of interest that Hutton speaks of Bagehot as 'at that time sharing his mother's Orthodoxy'; it may be that the nonconformist spirit, in this unanimously Unitarian *milieu*, led Bagehot to emphasise the Anglican side of his upbringing. Bagehot took advantage of his presence in the capital to attend, while at University College, various political meetings, hearing with admiration W. J. Fox and O'Connell and, in general, wallowing in the anti-Corn Law interest. Bagehot was every inch a townsman and a banker's son. Hutton of course was of the same mind in the matter of politics. He writes to Bagehot in September, 1843, on the subject of Cobden: 'from his voting with a small minority so consistently in favour of all the liberal motions, from seeing his name among the supporters of Mr. Roebuck's motion "that in all public schools supported by the state secular education only should be given and the religious left to the wish of the children's parents", from seeing his name in all the divisions against the Irish arms bill, and from his support of Mr. Christie's motion in favour of the admission of Dissenters to Cambridge, and last, but not least, his support of Mr. Sharman Cranford in his motion for an extension of the suffrage to the people, I should say he would be likely to extend to all other subjects that enlightened and liberal spirit which he is now showing in his

patriotic (in the true use of the word) exertions to root out monopoly from this country.'[1]

With Hutton, as with Roscoe, his other close friend at this
time, Bagehot seems to have established a pre-eminence which was
as much temperamental as intellectual. It is reported by his biographer—not perhaps without the partiality of a relative—that he
was 'a sort of demigod' among his fellow-students. Mrs. Barrington attributes this to a touch of 'wild reckless Cavalier spirit' in
her subject, traceable to royalist ancestors, for she seems to have
forgotten the more cautious enterprise of the Stuckeys. 'The
rollicking element was very refreshing when felt to be but an
offshoot of a passionately religious nature, of a delightful character,
of a sound understanding, and of a personal refinement quite
remarkable. If his friends could not rollick themselves, they
could be fascinated by rollicking in such a companion.'[2] Certainly
Bagehot has not lacked adulators. One, after his death, speaking
of the non-completion of the *Economic Studies*, even said: 'No
event could more powerfully suggest the notion of a life beyond
life, so as to explain the mystery of so fair a work being left
incomplete.'[3] Some kind of a hero this man certainly was. 'The
choice for a man', he wrote to Hutton in 1847, 'is whether he will
believe in God and duty, or whether he will believe in nothing.'[4]
Bagehot was, in some sense, a bold spirit, perhaps his contemporaries' idea of a bold spirit. He was, one may easily imagine,
more daring, and more amusing, than Hutton or Roscoe, but when
he kicked over the traces he did so gently. There is a passage in the
essay on Butler (1854) which shows how conscious he was of the
limitations on religious discourse in his age and *milieu*. 'At no
meeting of the higher classes, certainly none where ladies are
present, is there a tenth part of the plain questioning and *bona
fide* discussion of primary Christian topics, that there was at the

[1] Quoted in Barrington, *Life*, pp. 116–17.
[2] Barrington, *Life*, p. 114.
[3] Sir Robert Giffen, the *Fortnightly Review*, 1 April, 1880, quoted in Barrington,
Life, pp. 449–50.
[4] Letter quoted in Barrington, *Life*, p. 167.

select suppers of Queen Caroline.'[1] The French Revolution had
'frightened the English people' and scepticism had become 'an
ungentlemanly frame of mind'. Bagehot clearly envied Butler his
'daily familiarity with sceptical men'.[2] He quotes Butler to the
effect that it had come to be 'taken for granted by many persons
that Christianity is not so much a subject of inquiry, but that it is
now at length discovered to be false', and comments regretfully:
'No-one would so describe the tone of talk now. . . . Among
gentlemen a clergyman has scarcely the chance' of rashly entering
the lists with questioners. Bagehot does, however, pursue his
argument to the verge of what might have been regarded as
being ungentlemanly, but in such form that he appeared to be
talking religion rather than scepticism. The nature of revelation
is not a subject on which a patently sceptical person would waste
much breath unless, indeed, he were out to bait the religious, as
in our time or Butler's a Christian might feel inclined to bait the
irreligious. Bagehot has much to say on the subject, and a clear *a
priori* notion of what it should contain. 'In the first place', he says,
'so far from its being probable that Revelation would have con-
tained the same difficulties as Nature, we should have expected
that it would explain those difficulties. The very term Supernatural
Revelation implies that previously and by nature man is, to a
great extent, in ignorance; that particularly he is unaware of some
fact, or series of facts, which God deems it fit that he should
know. The instinctive presumption certainly is, that those facts
would be most important to us.'[3] The clear innuendo is that
what passes for the Christian revelation is not of this character.
'No one who reasons on this subject is likely to doubt that the
faculties of man are more clearly adequate to our daily and
temporal happiness, than to the explanation of the perplexities
which have confounded men since the beginning of speculation
. . . which relate to the scheme of the universe and the plan of God
. . . The advocate of revelation is for ever denying the competency
of man's faculties to explain, or puzzle out, what in the large

[1] *Works*, I, p. 279.   [2] *Works*, I, p. 280.   [3] *Works*, I, p. 292.

sense most concerns him. There are difficulties celestial, and difficulties terrestrial; but it is certainly more likely that God would interfere miraculously to explain the first than to remove the second.'[1] One senses a rather sharp distinction, in the back of Bagehot's mind, between the Sunday matters which are God's business and the Stock Exchange business he had better keep his nose out of. He goes on to illustrate the value of 'celestial' revelation by reference to the Atonement. There are divines who 'think, it is impossible to explain the mode in which the death of Christ conduces to the forgiveness of sin, or why a belief in it should be made, as they think it is, a necessary preliminary to such forgiveness. They consider that this is a revealed matter of fact; part of a system of things which is not known now, which would very likely be above our understanding if it were explained, which, at all events, is not explained.'[2] Things are not really allowed to be above Bagehot's understanding, any more than the landed gentry were allowed to be above the Bagehots and the Stuckeys. So much for the Atonement: 'so far as we can see, there was no occasion for it; it helps in nothing, explains to us nothing. . . . Such a revelation is, as has been said, possible; but it is much more likely, *a priori*, that a revelation, if given, would be a revelation of facts suited to our comprehension, and throwing light on the world in which we are.' Perhaps the Sunday world was superfluous after all, and the banker's world is the only real one. One can image that, with such discourse, Bagehot was able to impress with his speed and daring.

The education Thomas Bagehot wished to give his son was not to be ended with a bachelor's degree. Bagehot left Dr. Hoppus's establishment and went into lodgings to read for his M.A. The bachelor's degree had not been obtained without a break for ill-health—the autumn term of 1843 had been spent at Langport, where the cure seems to have been hacking, hunting and of course sympathy. The price of the master's degree, in 1848, was not less. Bagehot 'was in so weak a state that he had to lean

---

[1] *Works*, I, p. 293.   [2] *Works*, I, p. 295.

on a friend's arm when he went up to receive the gold medal'.[1]
Bagehot had by now not only established himself as a brilliant
student but begun to show his real turn of mind. Besides Hume
and Kant he had, Hutton says, 'mastered for the first time those
principles of political economy which were to receive so much
illustration from his genius in later years.'[2] Although, as Hutton
tells us, Shakespeare, Keats, Shelley and others including Mar-
tineau and John Henry Newman, were interspersed in Bagehot's
reading at this time, his first article, published in 1848, was on
The Currency Monopoly.[3] This was a review of three books or
pamphlets, among them a collection from the *Economist*, into
which institution Bagehot later had the discrimination to marry.
His second article, published in the same year, was a review of
Mill's *Principles of Political Economy.*[4] Both are long, able productions which have more behind them than the reading of a
student. Indeed they had behind them not only Bagehot's talent
but the Bristol and Somersetshire Bank which had turned into
Stuckey's Banking Company and already eaten up local banks in
Frome, Crewkerne, Yeovil, Bridgwater, Wells, Glastonbury,
Shepton Mallet, Taunton and Bath—to say nothing of Bristol.
All this was directed from the Stuckey-Bagehot headquarters in
Langport. The note issue was then or shortly afterwards to become the largest after that of the Bank of England. It provided
for Bagehot's monetary reflections a basis more solid than
theory.

After the M.A. and the Gold Medal for intellectual and moral
philosophy, Bagehot spent four years reading for the Bar in
suitably distinguished chambers. Before he was through he once
again became 'very unwell mentally and bodily', on his own
description, and, with what his sister-in-law calls 'the usual knack
he had of knowing what was the best thing to do under difficulties',[5] he went off for a long holiday in Paris. His friend Clough

---

[1] Barrington, *Life*, p. 181.
[2] R. H. Hutton, *Memoir*, in *Works*, I, p. 11.
[3] *Works*, VIII, p. 146
[4] *Works*, VIII, p. 188.   [5] Barrington, *Life*, p. 188-9

had found himself wandering through Europe in the revolutionary year 1848: Bagehot managed to be in Paris for Louis Napoleon's *coup d'état*. It was a part of his education the bank manager at Langport may not have foreseen, but it was certainly crucial. The high spirits of the *Letters on the Coup d'État*[1] show how effective a cure was the sight of other people at the barricades. If the bank gave solidity to Bagehot's speculations about the currency monopoly, the months in Paris in 1851-52 certainly sharpened his political perceptions. They also sharpened his sense of the pleasures of authorship. He decided that the law would not give him the leisure he required for this pursuit and, as soon as he had been called to the Bar, he withdrew to his father's counting-house in Langport. The exponent of the virtues of competition was thus shielded from any too strenuous exercise in that kind. It is from this date, 1852, that Bagehot's regular career as a writer really dates.

As Stuckey's bank provided the financial facilities for Bagehot's career as an author, it was his family's religious connections which ensured his easy *entrée* into the periodicals he needed. The *Letters on the Coup d'État* appeared in the weekly *Inquirer*. Bagehot's first articles, on political economy, had been published in the *Prospective Review*. It was in the *Prospective Review*, and later the *National Review*, that most of Bagehot's articles appeared until he got his teeth into the *Economist*. These were all Unitarian papers. The *Prospective* and the *National* are described by the historian of Unitarianism as the organs of the liberal wing of the movement which was 'largely made up of old Dissenting families, county landholders, and men engaged in business or commerce, predominating in London and the larger provincial towns, persons of moderate or large wealth and good education, inheriting the traditions of the old Presbyterianism.'[2] Bagehot, with his old friend Hutton, had a large part in starting up the *National Review*, though others, it seems, had to find the money,

[1] *Works*, I, pp. 77-137 (*E*. IV, 29).
[2] Earl Morse Wilbur, *A History of Unitarianism in Transylvania, England and America*, Cambridge, Mass., 1952, p. 369.

and directing and writing for it were 'among his chief occupations' from 1855 to 1864.[1] Bagehot was very broad-minded in his direction of the journal. 'I think certainly', he wrote to Hutton in 1856,[2] 'I should not reject an article for assuming the Deity of Christ.' In the same letter: 'There is a man Fitzjames Stephen . . . whom we should try to get hold of.' James Fitzjames Stephen, so admirable in exposition, puts what seems to have been Bagehot's theological position in a clearer light than Bagehot himself ever managed to do. With Stephen, Christianity finds a respected place almost on a level with rationalism. 'The new order of things which we see growing up in all directions', he writes, '–lay government, lay science, natural religion–are positive and living if ever anything was. The new elements introduced into life by Christianity itself, were not more full of vital energy and reality, than those which have been fostered and partially thrown into shape, by the movements of the last three centuries.'[3] It was Bagehot's mission to help to shape these elements more fully.

[1] Barrington, *Life*, p. 219.
[2] Barrington, *Life*, p. 221.
[3] Sir James Fitzjames Stephen, *Horae Sabbaticae*, Third Series, Macmillan, London, 1892, p. 304.

CHAPTER TWO

Essays and Elections

It was in the eighteen-fifties, during Bagehot's first main period as a writer, that most of his literary essays–or essays on literary subjects–were produced. The studies of Shakespeare, Cowper and Shelley all belong to this period. If was as if, in setting up as an author, he forgot his starting-point in the currency monopoly. No doubt there was in him at this time a genuine conflict of interests. When he died, in 1877, he had long been mainly occupied with *The English Constitution*, *Physics and Politics*, *Lombard Street* and *Economic Studies*. Mrs. Barrington believed that, 'before the end', he was 'rather reverting to earlier grooves of thought, and that, had he lived, he would have included in his future writings a class of subjects and impressions which characterised many of his earlier essays in the days before his life had become somewhat choked with business.' To some extent it may be we have here a reflection, in a domestic *milieu*, of the tired man of affairs. It is an aspiration not seldom expressed by people who prefer business and busy themselves about it, sometimes needlessly, that they will read a book when they retire. But Mrs Barrington is emphatic: 'He was getting impatient, I think, of having to devote his best energies to matters from which religion, poetry, and art'–those three luxuries of the true man of affairs–'were excluded. His connection with the Metaphysical Society to which Manning, Ward and Tennyson belonged, re-awakened trains of thought and speculation more in harmony with the trend of his feelings in those early days when Shelley and Keats were first delicious to him, and when Wordsworth and John Henry Newman were his daily food.'[1] There is another view. Herbert Read, who devoted a laudatory essay to Bagehot, concluded that 'it is doubtful if that intellect would ever have returned to pure literature: some psychological inhibition seems to have intervened and reformed his interests.'[2]

One of his later literary essays, that on *Mr. Clough's Poems*, was by way of being an act of piety. Clough was dead, and he had had, according to Hutton, 'a greater intellectual fascination for Bagehot than any of his contemporaries'.[3] It was in connection with University Hall, of which Clough became principal when he took refuge from Oxford, that the two became well acquainted. Bagehot was an active member of the council of that institution at one time, and claims to have helped Clough to the job. Certainly he seems to have played the part of the intellectual man of the world who could help the rather difficult poet, seven years his senior, to conduct himself in a manner acceptable to responsible people. Hutton puts it that Bagehot 'saw a good deal of Clough, and did what he could to mediate between that enigma to Presbyterian parents—a college head who held himself serenely neutral on almost all moral and educational subjects interesting to parents and pupils, except the observance of disciplinary rules—and the managing body who bewildered him and were by him bewildered. I don't think,' Hutton goes on, 'either Bagehot or Clough's other friends were very successful in their mediation, but he at least gained in Clough a cordial friend, and a theme of profound intellectual and moral interest to himself which lasted him his life, and never failed to draw him into animated discussion long after Clough's own premature death; and I think I can trace the effect which some of Clough's writings had on Bagehot's mind to the very end of his career.'[4] One difference Hutton noted between the two men was that Bagehot 'very quickly evacuated embarrassing positions, and never returned to them'. Clough on the other hand was tenacious of what he held to be the truth,

---

[1] Barrington, *Life*, p. 8.
[2] Herbert Read, *Collected Essays in Literary Criticism*, Faber, London, 1938, p. 313.
[3] R. H. Hutton, *Memoir*, in *Works*, I, p. 20.   [4] Hutton, *loc. cit.*

embarrassing or not–indeed it must sometimes have seemed, especially when it was embarrassing. Charles Whibley says he was 'one to whom no licence was permitted. The very candour of his mind made him suspect. If he looked over a gate, it was quite clear that he had stolen a horse'.[1] One imagines that, when Bagehot looked over a gate, people were apt to take him for the owner. He might, in fact, be considering whether to withdraw the owner's overdraft.

Bagehot's essay on Clough exhibits his own turn of mind very clearly. He appears as nothing less than the mediator between Christ and the divinities of Olympus. This is an advance even on acting as a go-between between Clough and the council of University Hall. Bagehot puts it plainly enough. 'The divinities of Olympus were in a very plain and intelligible sense part and parcel of this earth: they were better specimens than could be found below, but they belonged to extant species; they were better editions of visible existencies; they were', he goes on, warming to his subject, 'like the heroines whom young men imagine after seeing the young ladies of their vicinity.'[2] He contrasts with these 'the God of whom Christ speaks–the God who has not been seen at any time, whom no man hath seen or can see, who is infinite in nature, whose ways are past finding out.'[3] He goes on: 'The best of us'–Bagehot was always one of those–'strive, more or less, to "make the best of both worlds.". . . This is, as it seems, the best religion for finite beings, living, if we may say so, on the very edge of two dissimilar worlds.'[4] The insolence, not to say silliness, of Bagehot's solution, would leave one astounded, if one did not recall that the denial of the Incarnation was the cardinal doctrine of the kind of religion preached at Herd's Hill. Then comes Bagehot's characterisation of Clough. 'There are, however, some minds'– in contrast to his own–'which will not accept what appears to be an intellectual destiny. They struggle against the limitations of mortality, and will not condescend to use the natural and needful

---

[1] *Poems of Arthur Hugh Clough*, Macmillan, London, Sixth Edition, 1913, with an introduction by Charles Whibley, p. xxxiii.

[2] *Works*, IV, p. 115 (*E.* II, 241).   [3] *ibid.*   [4] *ibid.*, p. 116

aids of human thought. . . . They feel, and they rightly feel, that every image, every translation, every mode of conception by which the human mind tries to place before itself the Divine mind, is imperfect, halting, changing. . . . No one knows more certainly and feels more surely that there is an invisible world.'[1] At the same time 'the actual visible world as it was, and as he saw it,' exercised over Clough 'a compulsory influence. . . . Reconcile what you have to say with green peas, for green peas are certain; such was Mr. Clough's idea.'[2] There is no doubt that Bagehot was baffled as well as irritated by this mind so much more subtle, and more radical, than his own. 'Clough's chief fascination for Bagehot was, I think,' says Hutton, 'that he had as a poet in some measure rediscovered, at all events realised, as few ever realised before, the enormous difficulty of finding truth.'[3] That is better criticism than any in Bagehot's own essay. The nearest Bagehot comes to it is: 'His intellect moved with a great difficulty, and it had a larger inertia than any other which we have ever known.'

One has only to turn to Clough's own work to understand Bagehot's worry. It is not merely that the author of *The Bothie of Tober-Na-Vuolich* obviously knew the use of language in a manner utterly beyond Bagehot's reach. Even as a critic, as the notes on Dryden's English show, he clearly had the edge on the banker. He saw that the age suffered having no 'manner' suitable to its 'new matter'.[4] These sensitivities, one might say the vulnerability of his mind, gave his approach to religion a different turn from Bagehot's tactical rationalism. He might say, writing to his employers at University Hall, that his own feeling about prayer was 'to leave it, as I understand the Quakers do, to spontaneous emotion',[5] but he could also say of 'the new High Churchites, who want to turn all the quiet people adrift': 'it is the *New Plot*; but so long as one isn't obliged to sign articles, or go to daily service, or prayer-meeting, or the like, I don't see why one should excommunicate oneself. As for the Unitarians, they're better than

[1] *ibid.*, p. 117.   [2] *ibid.*, p. 119.   [3] Hutton, *Memoir*, in *Works*, I, p. 22.
[4] Arthur Hugh Clough, *The Poems and Prose Remains*, Macmillan, London, 1869, Vol. I, p. 332.   [5] A. H. Clough, *loc. cit.* p. 137.

the other Dissenters, and that's all; but go to their chapels,—no!'[1]
Elsewhere: 'I am convinced again that the Unitarian is morally
and religiously only half educated compared with the Episcopalian.
Modern Unitarianism is, I conceive, unfortunate on the one hand
in refusing to allow its legitimate force to the exercise of reason
and criticism; on the other hand, in having by its past exercise
of reason and criticism thrown aside treasures of pure religious
tradition because of their dogmatic exterior.'[2] But perhaps in *The
Latest Decalogue* Clough followed Bagehot still further into the
arcana of his religion:

> 'Thou shalt have one God only; who
> Would be at the expense of two?
> No graven images may be
> Worshipped, except the currency:
> Swear not at all; for, for thy curse
> Thine enemy is none the worse:
> At church on Sunday to attend
> Will serve to keep the world thy friend:
> Honour thy parents; that is, all
> From who advancement may befall;
> Thou shalt not kill; but need'st not strive
> Officiously to keep alive:
> Do not adultery commit;
> Advantage rarely comes of it:
> Thou shalt not steal; an empty feat,
> When it's so lucrative to cheat:
> Bear not false witness; let the lie
> Have time on its own wings to fly:
> Thou shalt not covet, but tradition
> Approves all forms of competition.'[3]

That surely is a portrait of Bagehot?

[1] A. H. Clough, *loc. cit.*, p. 135.   [2] A. H. Clough, *loc. cit.*, p. 425.
[3] A. H. Clough, *loc. cit.*, Vol. II, p. 186.

Walter Bagehot's interest in literature was, as much as anything, an interest in people. His literary essays do not take one far into the methods or peculiar ends of literature: the manner of his own writing shows that he had not the sort of relationship with words which is necessary for entry into such subjects. This deficiency does not signify merely a lack of interest in literary fripperies; it is a limitation of his penetration. It is the superficial social man which interests him—an amusing, even instructive, subject but one which has its full depth only when backed by the sort of curiosity about *man*, the sort of apprehension of his further reaches, which the voice of literature represents. Two of Bagehot's early literary essays—that on Hartley Coleridge and that on Shakespeare—illustrate this point. Most of what he has to say about Hartley Coleridge is about what he considered to be his social peculiarities. Hartley was one of those 'who never get on; whom the earth neglects, and whom tradesmen little esteem; who are where they were; who cause grief, and are loved; that are at once a by-word and a blessing; who do not live in life, and it seems will not die in death.'[1] Bagehot asserted that 'in few things do people differ more than in their perfect and imperfect realisation of this earth.'[2] There is no doubt that he regarded himself as a man who realised this world to perfection, and in a sense he was so, differing from the unfortunate Hartley to whom life was 'a floating haze, a disputable mirage: you must not treat him', he says, 'like a believer in stocks and stones—you might as well say he was a man of business.'[3] That Hartley did not do anything— of a kind Bagehot could recognise as being anything—was the subject of puzzled reproach more than once in the course of the essay. Hartley's 'outward life was a simple blank'. He walked around, talked to farmers in the Lake District; sometimes he talked to undergraduates or to women, but he did not do any- thing noticeable such as running a bank. 'There are undoubtedly persons', says Bagehot—and there is a wealth of experience behind his words—'who, though in general perfectly sane, and even with

[1] *Works* I, p. 188 (*E.* I, 143)   [2] *ibid.*, p. 190.   [3] *ibid.*, p. 192.

superior powers of thought or fancy, are as completely unable as the most helpless lunatic to manage any pecuniary transactions.'[1] Hartley was one of these. No wonder there was nothing to tell of him in thirty years! The superior genius of Shakespeare, on the other hand, is proved by nothing so much as his extreme prudence. His success was not so much in writing the plays as in investing money into a successful playhouse and thus being able to return to Stratford and make the local citizens treat him with respect.[2] There is a certain contempt for the mere poet, the mere intellectual, throughout Bagehot's literary essays. The 'tendency to, and the faculty for, self-delineation' which Bagehot not merely finds characteristic of Hartley Coleridge but of which he finds traces, for example, in Gray, is 'very closely connected with' 'dreaminess of disposition and impotence of character'. 'Persons very subject to these can grasp no external object, comprehend no external being; they can do no external thing, and therefore they are left to themselves.'[3] Bagehot's insistence on these points is very marked. There can be no doubt that it represents the anxiety of a man who has to bustle to prove his worth.

A similar concern shows itself in the essay on Cowper. There is the same crying up of the man of the world, as if every man were not a man of *some* world, and a singular air of patronage towards a writer who was, after all, the source of a stream of limpid English which represents a very high development of the intelligence. There is about Bagehot's discussion of Cowper's nervous disorders something which looks like brutality, but may have been partly the revulsion of one who was acquainted with madness in his own family and must have had occasion to speculate as to how far he was himself at risk. He introduces the subject with a hurrah for marriage and money, either of which 'breaks the lot of literary and refined inaction once and for ever'.[4] He goes on to say how 'singularly fortunate' Cowper's position was, because he had the choice of several lucrative public offices,

---

[1] *ibid.*, p. 204.
[3] *ibid.*, p. 211.
[2] See *Shakespeare–the Man, ibid.*, p. 219ff. (*E.* I, 173).
[4] *Works*, II, p. 13 (*E.* I, 263).

where the work required no ability, instead of having to meet 'the long labours of an open profession'. The tone is that of a merito-crat, though it was not only merit which gave Bagehot his entrée into the bank or into the *Economist*. 'It seemed at first scarcely possible that even the least strenuous of men should be found unequal to duties so little arduous or exciting.'[1] It is a curiously unsympathetic way of talking, for anyone who has read Cowper's own account of his apprehensions. There is a falsifying lack of sympathy, too, in Bagehot's account of Cowper's life at Olney, as it is reflected in *The Task*, as if the meaning of the poet's haven entirely escaped him. It is not the house on the market-place, with its incessant screaming of children and barking of dogs and the miserably poor inhabitants of the adjoining lane, that Bagehot has in mind, but the Victorian comfort of the house at Herd's Hill, when he says: 'Have we not always hated this life? What can be worse than regular meals, clock-moving servants, a time for everything, and everything then done . . .' And there is something of Bagehot's rather nasty contempt for ordinary people in what follows about 'a common gardener, a slow parson, a heavy assortment of near relations'. A 'placid house flowing with milk and sugar–all that the fates can stuff together of substantial comfort, and fed and fatted monotony';[2] that surely reflects Bagehot's life rather than Cowper's. And so it is perhaps of the paternal Unitarianism, rather than of the Puritan Trinitarianism which was Cowper's religion, that Bagehot is thinking when he says that 'a prolonged meditation on unseen realities seems scarcely an occupation for which common human nature was intended'[3] or that 'it seems hardly possible that an imagination such as Cowper's . . . should leave its own home–the *domus et tellus*– the sweet fields and rare orchards which it loved–to go out alone apart from all flesh into the trackless and fearful unknown Infinite.'[4]

---

[1] *ibid.*, p. 14.   [2] *ibid.*, p. 34.   [3] *ibid.*, p. 26.   [4] *ibid.*, p. 27.

Throughout Bagehot's literary essays the same preoccupations recur. Literature is an avenue to subjects which interest him more. He might have said—in various forms did say—that the author interested him more than the book. There is a sense in which that is the proper end of all such studies. In the best critics the man is weighed through the book. This is the case, patently, in Johnson's *Lives of the Poets*; it is also the case, though less obviously, in the technical criticism of Ezra Pound. Bagehot's interest is of a different, and much more superficial kind. He does not seek out the idiosyncrasy, or the genius, the particular tone or cadence which gives an author his value, in order to understand what possibilities of the human mind are peculiarly represented by the author he is studying. He stops short, through sheer incapacity, of any such wide apprehension of his subject and sets up instead a commonplace figure with which he can amuse his public and demonstrate his own abilities. The essay on Shakespeare is a blatant example of this. No doubt Shakespeare was glad to make some money, and we hope he did, but the abilities of this kind which Shakespeare may have had in common with Bagehot are not what make him Shakespeare. A critic who helps us with an obscure point in the text, or who throws light on the structure of a sonnet, does more for our understanding of the poet than all Bagehot's dashing essay can do. Bagehot lacked patience and humility before his subjects as well as any technical grasp of what his poets were up to. The superficiality of his performance as a literary critic was well pointed by Keynes, who also diagnosed the cause of it. 'Bagehot', he said in the review of the *Collected Works* he published in *The Economic Journal* in 1915,[1] 'was a psychologist—a psychological analyser, not of the great or of genius, but of those of a middle position, and primarily of business men, financiers and politicians.' In fact the analysis, as is usually the case, was primarily of himself, and it stopped short of what could be unflattering to such a man.

---

[1] J. M. Keynes, 'The Works of Bagehot', *The Economic Journal*, September 1915, p. 369.

It is indeed characteristic of Bagehot in his literary essays that he sets up, not man as the measure of all things but the mere man of affairs as the measure of his betters. In a sense he could not help this, for he was himself that mere man of affairs, only endowed with a certain facility of pen which is not to be taken for granted in such people, though the weakness is more common than it was in Bagehot's day. It is not merely individual authors, but the collective achievements of the human mind, that he looks at in this way. There is something supercilious about the way in which Bagehot talks of 'the simple *naïveté* of the old world' in his essay on *Béranger*.[1] He thrusts forward comforts of middle-class Victorian life with a snigger, saying they 'may or may not be great benefits according to a recondite philosophy' and knowing that he will have the support of all decent mediocrities in putting at the centre of the intellectual stage what belongs to the periphery. It is of a piece with this that, while praising the admirable Béranger, he has by implication to take a swipe at Racine as not exhibiting 'the higher freedom of the impelling imagination'.[2]

It is in the essay on *Wordsworth, Tennyson and Browning* (1864) that Bagehot comes nearest to putting forward a theory of literature. The essay is also Bagehot's farewell to literary studies. After that the other interests which already dominated him took over exclusively, so far as the writer was concerned. In this essay Bagehot propounds a literary theory which has all the characteristics of shoddiness and showiness which one comes to expect in his work. After a disquisition on the *picturesque*, in relation to painting—which is really a discourse on the mid-Victorian consumer's notion of what a picture should be like—he invents the rather tasteless word *literatesque* to describe the same quality in relation to writing. It stands for 'that perfect combination in *subject-matter* of literature, which suits the *art* of literature'.[3] There are the people who would look well in a book and the people who would not. Those who would are not necessarily the

---

[1] *Works* III, pp. 5ff. (*E*. II, 11).
[2] *ibid*., p. 12.　　　　　　[3] *Works* IV, p. 272 (*E*. II, 321).

41

best people, but they are 'the most effective'. This is virtually a recipe for the ordinary trade novel, in Bagehot's day or in our own. Bagehot's notions of literature, fundamentally, are those of Lord Jeffrey, about whom he had written some years before in his essay on *The First Edinburgh Reviewers* (1855).[1] Jeffrey derided Wordsworth for having produced work which was not *literatesque*, by the standards of the ordinary educated taste of his day By Bagehot's day Wordsworth has been taken into the system. The expectation of the ordinary educated reader had changed, but the system of recommending whatever is in accordance with his expectations, in a bright and knowing way which confirms the reader's confidence in his own ingenuity, is the same with Bagehot as with Jeffrey. This system is now all but universal and there is generally no difference between the literary pages of newspapers and periodicals and the pages devoted to fashions in clothes or in food and wine. Bagehot's more refined ideas are of an extraordinary vulgarity. He talks of the greatest artists as showing 'an enthusiasm for reality'.[2] One has only to think of Dr. Johnson to get the measure of that phrase, which combines a silly notion of enthusiasm with an ordinary busy-body's notion of reality. When one finds that Ben Jonson is classed as one who lacked the qualifying enthusiasm, lived on 'the parings of the intellect' and was unable to grasp the 'real world' of Vincent Stuckey, one has the measure of Bagehot as a literary critic.

In the biographical essays Bagehot undoubtedly shows his talent to better advantage, and more particularly when he was dealing with a mind well within his own scope. The various men of affairs he wrote about were the best subjects for him, not merely because it was in the affairs of money and bustle that his heart lay but because his condescending manner becomes him best when he is writing about someone who has intellect enough genuinely to condescend to. The study in which Bagehot shows us most of his own mind is perhaps that on *The Character of Sir Robert Peel*. He stood just far enough back from Peel, in intellectual perspectives

---

[1] *Works*, II, pp. 51ff. (*E*. I, 309). [2] *Works*, *IV*, p. 273.

as well as in time. He starts his study with a reflection on the pastness of the past which has the colour of his habitual thoughts. We look over old letters, he says, and are surprised to find that what seemed important then no longer is so, and that people believed then things we do not believe now and revolved questions which for us are no longer questions at all. The illustration he gives is the question of what was called 'Catholic emancipation', which agitated the world in Peel's day and on which Peel, like so many other slow-moving men, took first one side and then the other, ending, of course, on what was proving to be the popular side and became the course of history. 'Who now doubts on the Catholic Question?' asks Bagehot. 'It is no longer a "question".'[1] It is as if Bagehot were saying, looking back over a series of old prints, 'What funny clothes they wore!' Yet Bagehot, it is to be remembered, is the advocate of the reality of the actual. He is the man who asserts repeatedly that what ordinary men, and above all men of business, are about day by day is of a seriousness which puts in the shade the frivolities of mere intellect or mere religion. With the passage of time – even of a little time – the reality of these great affairs fades to nothing, but we are invited to believe that what is currently held to be important – the new candidate for the attention of practical men – is very much *something*. The approach is the opposite of that of a Burke or a Swift, who are holding fast to something permanent and, without relaxing their hold on the business of the day, are able to see it as a manifestation of more permanent interests. Bagehot has the effrontery to speak else-where[2] of 'a clever affectation of commonsense . . . in all Swift's political writings' and to contrast the Dean of St. Patrick's unfavourably with Sidney Smith, another buoyant character with a grip of iron on reality, according to Bagehot, while Swift perhaps 'had no heart' and was not sympathetic to bankers. No doubt the question of the civil rights of Roman Catholics in England is not one that could be tactfully broached again in

[1] *Works*, II, p. 178 (*E*. III, 241).
[2] In the essay on 'The First Edinburgh Reviewers', *Works*, II, p. 83.

Bagehot's day, any more than it could be in our own, but it is not a matter for astonishment that it was once thought important. Indeed, it is a question so deeply implicated in our history that it does not die and has not become insignificant, merely changed its form. Bagehot's corrosive views on religion, which dismissed the claims of the Church of England and welcomed the Italian-Irish intervention not for its truth but as something which gave him another card to be played off against orthodoxy, naturally inclined him to see merely the question of political expediency. Once that was out of the way, there was no question at all, for him. One opinion was as good as another and reality was not implicated in the argument at all. Sensible men of business had long concluded that such matters should not stand in the way of the expansion of commerce.

'This world is given to those whom this world can trust,'[1] Bagehot says, and his cleverness was to take the world's side of the argument, the side of the winners against that of the losers. It is a version of the cynicism of Machiavelli, adapted to less dangerous times. Bagehot, of course, had none of the profound reserves entertained by the Florentine secretary, and he did not see the evil as evil. For his mind there was not truth and falsehood, apprehended with varying degrees of clarity, but a stream of opinions from which the clever man fished out the ones most likely to be acceptable to the world of the moment. There is of course sound observation of the world in all this. No doubt Bagehot had found, moving among men of business more slow-witted than himself, that to be too quick to seize the drift of things only aroused distrust. He probably found it difficult to hold his tongue and wait for the world to catch up, and it must have been a relief to move from what was once called the counting-house, and from the necessity of inspiring confidence in the dull-witted men who sought for loans, to the editorial desk of the *Economist* where it did no harm to be a little ahead of current opinion—but of course not too much, for a journalist would be out

[1] *Works*, II, p. 181.

44

of business even more quickly than a banker, if he exceeded the permitted tolerance in this matter and insisted on a point because it was true rather than because it was about to become the opinion of the day. Peel provided an ideal text for Bagehot's exposition of his particular form of realism. 'No man' Bagehot says, 'has come so near our definition of a constitutional statesman—the powers of a first-rate man and the creed of a second-rate man.' The statesman, of course, was a step behind the journalist, but in the same file. Peel was 'never in advance of his time. Of almost all the great measures with which he was associated, he attained great eminence as an opponent before he attained even greater eminence as their advocate. . . . He did not bear the burden and heat of the day; other men laboured, and he entered into their labours. As long as these questions remained the property of first-class intellects; so long as they were confined to philanthropists and speculators; as long as they were only advocated by austere, intangible Whigs' —observe the innuendo in favour of the opposite party—'Sir Robert Peel was against them. So soon as these same measures, by the progress of time, the striving of understanding, the conversion of receptive minds, became the property of second-class intellects, Sir Robert Peel became possessed of them also. He was converted at the conversion of the average man. His creed was, as it had ever been, ordinary; but his extraordinary abilities never showed themselves so much.'[1]

Bagehot remarks that Peel was fortunate in that 'the principal measures required in his age were "repeals". From changing circumstances, the old legislation would no longer suit a changed community; and there was a clamour, first for the repeal of one important Act, and then of another.'[2] This suited Peel's type of mind. It also characterises Bagehot's. The endless yielding to circumstance, until the merits of what is to be done matter nothing as compared with the dexterity required to get out of an awkward situation, has become so much a habit of mind, in the England of our own day, that the consequences of continuing in this line of

---

[1] *ibid.*, p. 183. [2] *ibid.*, p. 212.

behaviour are scarcely marked. It ends in the comfort of the operator being the only consideration which should determine action. This may be all right for a private banker, in his acquisitive field. It is something to be watched for rather than encouraged in a politician. There is of course a sense in which this sort of adjustment is an essential feature—*the* essential feature—of our sort of democracy and it has undoubtedly facilitated a number of social changes which were inseparable from the development of technology. It has retarded other changes and resulted in a number of disastrous decisions, simply because there are many circumstances in which there is no chance of acting sensibly if the timing has to be dependent on the applause of a sufficient number of people. Bagehot's view was that the paraphernalia of the constitution, of Church and Crown and Parliament, did not matter as long as the business of the day was done. It is a point of view so familiar to us that it is accepted by most people without a thought. The unimportance of everything except the promotion of manufacture and the circulation of money now seems to be as unquestionable truth as ever our former constitutional principles were. Indeed it has replaced those constitutional principles. It is a possibility that this truth may be open to question in its turn. But Bagehot, like Sir Robert Peel, moved in the happy atmosphere of destruction, with reserves however about the destruction of bankers and the removal of the carpet from under his own feet.

These reserves are evident in Bagehot's essay on *Parliamentary Reform* (1859). It seems astonishing now that, little over a hundred years ago, people were still debating not merely how far the franchise should go, but what the system of representation should be. Bagehot was writing at a time when both Whigs and Tories were 'pledged to do something' more about the franchises but when neither as a party had 'agreed what they should do'.[1] He was satisfied, in looking back, that the Reform Act of 1832 had been beneficial. Had it not reduced the influence of what he called elsewhere 'the morbidly agricultural counties'[2] and 'the

---

[1] *Works*, III, p. 108.   [2] *Works*, II, p. 182.

obscure abodes of squires and rectors'[1] and put power into the hands of 'the general aggregate of fairly instructed men'?[2] Opponents of the Bill had said ' "that the measure could not be final" ',[3] that there would be a movement for wider and wider enfranchisement until we had all the horrors of democracy. Bagehot, with the blandness so familiar to us in the comfortable English liberal denying the tendency of his actions, assured his readers that 'the reality is the reverse of the anticipation'.[4] It is not that Bagehot wanted to persuade people that there was little to fear, or that there might be advantages, in a movement towards universal franchise. He simply did not see it coming. He was against the 'ultra-democratic theory' that 'parliamentary representation should be "proportioned to mere numbers" '.[5] The main defect he saw in the electoral law after 1832 was an 'undue bias toward the sentiments and views of the landed interest'.[6] The surrounding fields always get poor treatment, in Bagehot's works, as compared with the businessmen of Langport. It was not in numbers of seats that the agricultural interest was favoured; the boroughs were in a strong majority over the countries. The trouble was the more insidious one of the prestige of the land-owning classes. People did not respect the bankers and manufacturers as much as they should have done. If they could make up to a duke with broad acres, or even a miserable squire, they preferred that. The result was too many landowners in public life, altogether too little deference to those whose money was in funds. Since for Bagehot a main merit of Parliament was its broad agreement with the sentiment of the country it is difficult to see why he should have objected to this lingering preference for the land. Or it should be difficult, if Bagehot's own principles are to be taken seriously.

Bagehot's proposal for improving the representative quality of the Commons was not to widen the franchise by any general extension, but to rearrange the system in a way which would

[1] *ibid.*, p. 190.
[3] *ibid.*, III, p. 112.
[5] *ibid.*, pp. 124–5.

[2] *Works*, III, p. 109.
[4] *ibid.*, p. 113.
[6] *ibid.*, p. 113.

produce the right answer from the point of view of sensible men of business like himself. It would be dangerous to submit the choice of rulers to the 'direct vote of the populace'. That would be to risk 'vulgarising the whole tone, method and conduct of public business,'[1] and to give 'entire superiority to the lower part of the community'.[2] The results of this would be 'beyond controversy pernicious'.[3] He saw intelligence as linked with the growth of property. If the poor inconsiderately increased in numbers, that did not matter, so far as the franchise was concerned. He wanted to secure representation for the working classes, but in such a way as would not upset the dominance of the property-owning classes. The 'nameless charm of refinement'[4] helped to keep the power where it should be, but Bagehot understandably did not rely too heavily on this. He would found working-class constituencies, but make sure there were not too many of them. The agricultural labourer, for whom he had a special contempt, could be ignored. The claim for equality of franchise across the country need not be taken seriously. Bagehot's scheme was to 'create *de novo* a beneficial variety of property qualifications'.[5] What qualified a man to vote in one constituency would not so qualify him in another. The solution was a kind of sham antique, not merely preserving but imitating the chaos which had come down from the miscellaneous local history of earlier times. The balance to be achieved was one which would give advantage to the money-making classes to which Bagehot belonged, and so to the growing parts of the economy. However antiquated the method, the objective Bagehot had in mind is one the modern reader will find familiar enough.

The essay on *Parliamentary Reform* throws a good deal of light on the meaning of Bagehot's political liberalism. It is of interest, too,

---

[1] *ibid.*, p. 129.   [2] *ibid.*, p. 125.   [3] *ibid.*, p. 126.
[4] *ibid.*, p. 121.   [5] *ibid.*, p. 153.

as showing how he applied himself to the theory of representation before trying the hustings himself.

Bagehot's major essay in practical politics was in the Bridgwater by-election of 1866. It was not a happy occasion for him. Practice proved to be less exhilarating than theory. Bagehot had given some thought to standing as a candidate for London University in 1860. In 1865 there had been some idea of his standing for Dudley and then for Manchester. In 1866, in Bridgwater, he saw the thing through to his defeat by seven votes at the hands of the Conservative candidate, Bagehot himself of course being the Liberal. The matter did not end there, however, nor with his unsuccessful attempt to get himself nominated for London University in 1867. In 1869 there was a Commission 'to inquire into the existence of Corrupt Practices at the last Election, and at previous elections' in Bridgwater and Bagehot had the opportunity of demonstrating how he had conducted himself.

It appears that there was some thought of nominating Bagehot in Bridgwater in the general election of 1865. He attributed the fact that he was in the end not then nominated to one of the promoters of the Liberal interest having an old feud with Stuckey's Bank. Be that as it may, he had been thought of before 1866 and when it became evident that there was to be a by-election, he was waited on in London by three gentlemen, Mr. Lovibond, Mr. Barham and Mr. Reed. Westropp, who had been declared elected at the general election, had just been unseated for bribery, and the understanding at this interview naturally was that 'the party had determined on their election being pure'. Bagehot remembered having said at the interview that he understood that the Liberals had been pure at the 1865 election, and that his interlocutors had said 'Oh, yes', though they certainly knew better. It needs a great charity to suppose that Bagehot, with his local knowledge, did not know better too. He was pressed on this point by the Commissioners who conducted the Inquiry in 1869. After he had been made to read before them his own declaration of high principles, and a motion carried by his supporters, one of the Commissioners asked:

'42,002[1] It appears therefore that they wish to have it go forth that their intention was equally pure with your own?—That is what I understood to be their intention.

'42,003 (*Mr. Coleridge.*) You say you understand, did you believe?—Oh, I believed. I believed it on this ground, that though I perfectly well knew in former times the Liberal party had been quite as bad as the other, yet having turned out Mr. Westropp for bribery, and the election having been pure in 1865, I considered I might rely on that pledge.

'42,004. But you are assuming a great deal in saying that they had been pure in 1865?—Well, that is what was stated to me.'

Whatever may have been the state of his knowledge of the proceedings in 1865, Bagehot had stated his own position quite unequivocally to the electors in 1866. The tone of low magnanimity may be pardoned, or at any rate borne with, on such an occasion:

'There is a remarkable class of people whose position in the matter I do not understand. I understand Mr. Westropp's, and I do not want to be hard upon him; after all, he has suffered a great penalty in being excluded from Parliament.' Bagehot might well understand Mr. Westropp's position. 'He was very ambitious of his seat, and therefore, had great temptation. I can, too, make allowance for the poor voter; he is, most likely, ill-educated, certainly ill off, and a little money is a nice bait to him. What he does is wrong, but it is intelligible. What I do not understand is the position of the rich, respectable, virtuous members of a party which countenances these things. (*Cheers.*) They are like the man who stole stinking fish, they commit a crime, and they get no benefit. (*Laughter*)' (41,998).

Bagehot's pre-nomination interview with Mr. Lovibond, Mr. Barham and Mr. Reed went on to a financial topic of which it was possible to speak openly, but which may have been the subject of some unspoken musings by at least some of the parties present. This was the question whether Bagehot would subscribe after-

---

[1] This and the following similarly numbered extracts are from the evidence accompanying the *Second Report of the Bridgwater Bribery Commission*, 1869.

wards to a petition against the malpractices of the other side, supposing he were defeated and the Conservative got in. Bagehot let it be known that he would be willing to put up something like £600 or £700 for such a purpose. Mr. Barham had thus satisfied himself that Bagehot was prepared to spend some money in connection with the election. Bagehot's next step seems to have been to take advice from a London solicitor, George Robins, as to what the legal limits of financial manoeuvre were, for a candidate. The evidence on this point is not very explicit. Robins said (41,255): 'When Mr. Bagehot first came to see me he wanted me, as a friend, to protect him in the matter: he did not know what might happen, and he should refer everybody to me.' There was a certain prospective anxiety on Bagehot's part. 'He might', Robins said, 'be led to spend money illegally, and that was his particular objection. Emphatically he said that.' (41,256). What Bagehot thought at this time about the state of the law was brought out in the Commissioners' examination (42,079). He thought that it was illegal to bribe in advance but that it was not an offence to do so retrospectively. What he gave Mr. Barham to understand, at the first interview in London, was that he 'would be quite liberal in everything that was legal' (41,980).

The Commissioners gave themselves the satisfaction of eliciting a statement from Bagehot about the view he would take of retrospective bribery before they came to the details of his own case. This must have been done with a view to what was to follow, and Bagehot was not quite sharp enough for them. Asked whether he would have been willing, when he went down to Bridgwater, to pay outstanding bills incurred by candidates in the earlier election, he said he would not: '41,992. I need hardly ask you, would you have repudiated that as much as any other form of bribery?–I should have repudiated it.'

What actually happened on 7 June, 1866, the day of the by-election, is variously told by the participants. The Commissioners' report sums up to the effect that, at 12 o'clock, the Conservative agent regarded the election as lost, 'but hearing that 30 voters were bottled at "The Bull and Butcher", he sent a note to Mr.

Bealey Smith, telling him that if he could let him have £300 he could poll 30 men. The money was sent, the men polled, and the election was won by a majority of 7. The numbers were for

Patton	301
Bagehot	294

7 majority.'

Bagehot's account of his feeling in the course of the polling day, as he watched for the effect of bribes on the other side, is as follows: 'I was told early in the morning by Mr. Lovibond that the money had not come down they had heard, and therefore he thought he should be able to congratulate me. I remember his coming into the room, and saying that, and for a long time I was in a considerable majority, but not more than I had a right to be probably. I do not know how long I was looking for the money of the other side to come and counteract this. That is what I had been expecting, but it did not come. I seemed to be getting ahead, and getting ahead, and then at last I saw what I had expected had come, but I cannot say the precise time.' (42,035) He had been glad to be in a minority, he informed the sceptical Commissioners, because he thought the majority would not have been honestly procured.

'42,034. You think you would not have felt any great sense of triumph if you had been returned, from what your feelings were? – I did not much care at all.'

Bagehot admitted to having suspected, in the course of the polling day, that someone was doing on his behalf 'what they ought not to do' and he said he became sure about this when, the election having been lost, nothing was said about a petition, and it was clear that the £600 he had promised would not be wanted for that purpose. He went back to Langport immediately after the result was declared, no doubt to wander moodily round the house on Herd's Hill. A day or two later he went back to Bridgwater. Mr. Barham and Mr. Lovibond came to see him and told him 'that money had been spent'. He cut them rather short.

He afterwards told the Commissioners, rather oddly, that he was not sure whether he said anything to indicate his disgust, but 'I looked it I know' (42,075). Anyway he referred Barham to Robins, as he had told Robins he would if there was trouble. It emerged at the Inquiry that Barham had drawn £700 in cash from what one of the Commissioners described as 'an imaginary account' at the West of England Bank in Bridgwater, at the time of the election, and the cashier gave evidence that he knew what the money was for and that he would have paid more–a couple of thousand pounds–if Barham had wanted it. Barham naturally followed up the instruction to go and see Robins after the election. Through this channel Bagehot paid up, the whole cost of the affair being £1,533 10s. 2d. as compared with his published expense of £193 10s. 2d. He said he thought it would not make a 'good moral impression' if he did not pay. It is a tenable point of view but, as one of the Commissioners suggested, possibly 'a violation of that pledge' Bagehot had given 'so admirably' in the words of the speech he had been made to read before them. Bagehot having been led on by the Commissioners, earlier in his examination, to repudiate the idea of retrospective bribery in connection with the candidates of the previous election, could only excuse himself feebly.

'I never knew the paying of money under such circumstances when bribery had taken place was a criminal offence at all, till the other day.

'42,080. Did it not strike you to be, whatever the law was, as complete an offence against the moral code as if you had previously authorised it?–I do not say it was right; that is another thing, but I thought you were asking me as to the law.'

There was something said in one of the newspapers to the effect that Bagehot's family had put up the money. Bagehot went out of his way to deny this before the Commissioners, and one can well believe that Thomas Bagehot would not have spent money on anything so frivolous as unsuccessful bribes. Bagehot was careful to say that he had paid the money on the advice of Mr. Robins. There is an emphasis which is not altogether pleasant, in the circumstances, about Bagehot's 'I entirely acted under his advice throughout' (42,102). Robins freely admitted that he had advised Bagehot to pay. Barham was even more engaging as to his part: 'I thought that was our fault entirely; we not only spent the money, but we made a mess of it.' (12,938)

One of the Commissioners suggested to Bagehot that it was 'with a view to keeping up an influence in the borough in the future' that he paid the money. Bagehot replied that this consideration 'did not operate in his mind at the time'. However that may be, he soon took to writing about the Constitution instead of trying to work a corner of it. *The English Constitution* was published in 1867. After the Bribery Commission's report Bagehot was, perhaps, not in a very strong position to seek further nominations. The finding was that he was 'privy and assenting to some of the corrupt practices extensively prevailing' at the by-election. He could still promote intelligent government from the editorial chair of the *Economist*.

The adventure in Bridgwater receives only a sidelong glance from Bagehot's official biographer. Indeed, it is hard to absolve Mrs. Barrington of disingenuousness, unless perhaps she relied entirely on the loyal Hutton for her account of what happened. At any rate her account of the affair, certainly largely derived from Hutton, is designed to leave the impression that Bagehot, his face set nobly against corruption, came off scot-free. She quotes a bit of the evidence in which he gives an account of evading a direct demand for a bribe–as any prudent candidate would do. The extract also shows Bagehot being very amusing– as Hutton thought–at the expense of 'these rustics' whose votes he wanted. No doubt what Bagehot said gave a substantially accurate version of what the elector in question said to him. He has, however, almost certainly tampered with the language. In his version what 'the rustic' said has the air of a caricature rather than of a mere report. It is in the style of a supercilious *Punch* joke about the lower orders. ' "I won't vote for gentlefolks unless they do something for I. Gentlefolks do not come to I unless they want something of I, and I won't do nothing for gentlefolks, unless they do something for me." [1] Mrs. Barrington quotes–from Hutton–the address to the Bridgwater Constituency which the members of the Commission had given themselves the pleasure of inviting Bagehot to read to them, evidently because it struck them as inconsistent with his actions, but she says nothing of the Commission's findings on the subject of Bagehot's conduct. Indeed she concludes her account of the episode by quoting Bagehot's own rather offensive comment on his examination. ' "You will like to hear that my reputation for ability is much raised at Bridgwater since my examination. They say, 'Ah! Mr. Bagehot was too many for them. They broke Westropp but they could not break him.' They regard it as a kind of skill, independent of fact or truth. 'You win if you are clever, and lose if you are stupid', is their idea at bottom." ' [2]

The electors' idea of 'skill, independent of fact or truth' was precisely Bagehot's own. The cynicism of his identification with the base pleasure of these simple practical men, the corrupt electors of Bridgwater, is an unguarded revelation made, no doubt, in a moment of excitement after an examination in which he had feared he might fare worse.

[1] Question 42,018 of the evidence in the *Second Report*, quoted by Mrs. Barrington in *Life*, p. 291.
[2] Barrington, *Life*, pp. 292–3.

CHAPTER THREE

Political Theories

Bagehot's *début* as a political writer was with the *Letters on the French Coup d'État of 1851*, which are a remarkable performance for a young man of twenty-six. Bagehot as yet had no experience of affairs, but by hereditary instinct or domestic training he managed to exhibit all the prudence of a man whose common sense would always get the better of him. He was of course writing for a Unitarian journal, and there is an extravagance in his manner which suggests that he was giving himself the pleasure of causing astonishment among its grave readers, as he had amused himself by daring thought in the presence of Richard Holt Hutton. He went to Paris because, subjectively, 'everything of all kinds had gone wrong' with him,[1] and he was bored with his apprenticeship in law; the release he felt shows in his exuberance. It was almost exactly at the time when a political writer of a different quality, P. -J. Proudhon, operating from his prison in the Conciergerie, was publishing *L'Idee générale de la Révolution au XIXe siècle*. No voice could be less like Bagehot's than Proudhon's was. 'The prejudice of government penetrates the depths of people's consciousness and stamps reason with its image, so that any other idea has long been made impossible, and the boldest of thinkers have arrived at the point of saying that government is a plague no doubt, a punishment for mankind, but that it is a necessary evil.'[2] In Proudhon's terms, Bagehot was one of those

---

[1] Barrington, *Life*, p. 189.
[2] P.-J. Proudhon, *Idée générale de la Révolution au XIXe siècle* Marcel Rivière, Paris, 1923, p. 183 (author's translation).

for whom government was instituted. He was one of the rich set over against the poor, of whom Proudhon was one, while he was himself one of those whom government protected in protecting property. The martyrdom of the proletariat was not the sort of idea which could enter Bagehot's head. It was not merely that he was on the side of the shop-keepers and against the artisans. While Proudhon, engaged in struggles which for most men would have been obsessive, was of a turn of mind which diverted him, repeatedly, from practical political action to matters of more permanent importance, Bagehot's energies swayed him like a magnetic needle in the direction of the money, however well his personal situation might provide for him to exercise the rôle of a disinterested philosopher. Bagehot had read some Proudhon, and was gracious enough to say that he wrote well. It is almost certain, however, that he did not realise the scope of Proudhon's thought or understand its importance. Bagehot thought in terms of immediate practical results, and he was right in judging that the populace was unlikely to follow a philosopher. But the philosopher was nearer to reality than the practical man. However little Proudhon approved of the mind of the *peuple* or, one might say more simply, the ordinary human mind, he understood it profoundly. 'Down to our day, the most emancipating revolutions, and all the effervescences of liberty, have regularly ended in an act of faith and of submission to power. . . . What has kept up this mental predisposition and made the fascination invincible for so long, is that, as a result of the supposed analogy between society and the family, the government has always presented itself to people's minds as the natural organ of justice, the protector of the weak, the keeper of the peace. By this attribution to government of the qualities of a providential guarantor, it took root in people's hearts as in their intelligences. It became part of the universal mind; it was the faith, the intimate and invincible superstition of the *citoyens*. If it showed signs of going wrong, people said of it, as of Religion and Property: it isn't the institution which is wrong, it is the abuse of it. It isn't the king who is bad, it is his ministers. *Ah! si le roi savait! . .*'

In writing his first letter, Bagehot was clearly addressing him-self to characteristic British liberal attitudes. Obviously to over-throw a republic was a very wicked act; obviously its perpetrator must be very unpopular. 'On the contrary,' says Bagehot, 'the President is, just now, really strong and really popular . . . the act of 2 December did succeed and is succeeding . . . many . . . most of the inferior people do really and sincerely pray *Domine Salvum fac Napoleonem.*' The 'inferior people' is a typical Bagehot conception; it means, of course, 'other and less important people'.[1] 'The political justification of Louis Napoleon,' he goes on, 'is to be found in the state of the public mind which immediately preceded the *coup d'état*. It is very rarely that a country expects a revolution at a given time.' But this time they did; ladies taking on new maids even chose them for their likely performance during calamity. 'The only notion of '52 was: *on se battra dans la rue.* Their dread was especially of socialism; they expected the fol-lowers of M. Proudhon, who advisedly and expressly maintains "anarchy" to be the best form of Government, would attempt to carry their theories into action.'[2]

Bagehot went into the streets and obviously enjoyed the exceptional tourist attractions of the moment. He saw 'men whose physiognomy . . . resembled the traditional Montagnard, sallow, stern, compressed . . . brooding one-idead thought . . . angry, armed to the teeth . . . gloomy fanatics, *over*-principled ruffians',[3] manning the barricades.

'I *felt* he would rather shoot me than not.' The unfriendliness obviously astonished him; where he came from, people had always treated his advances with respect. Here were men to whom it was no good to be affable! Bagehot concluded rapidly for the safe side of the argument. 'You will not be misled by any high-flown speculation about liberty or equality', he warns his Unitarian readers who, on their island and away from such *fracas* were apt to be precisely so misled. 'You will, I imagine, concede to me that the first duty of a Government is to ensure the security of that

---

[1] *Works*, I, p. 78. [2] *ibid.*, p. 80. [3] *ibid.*, p. 81.

industry which is the condition of social life and civilised cultivation . . . that no danger would be more formidable than six
months beggary among the revolutionary *ouvriers*.' It is evidently
the threat to the shop-keepers which worries him. 'It is from this
state of things,' he goes on, 'that Louis Napoleon has delivered
France. The effect was magical.' The best of it is, he adds, once
more no doubt with the idea of causing astonishment in the
respectable circles he was addressing, that the whole thing is
unconstitutional. 'No legal or constitutional act could have given
an equal confidence. What was wanted was an assurance of
audacious government, which would stop at nothing, scruple at
nothing, to secure its own power and the tranquillity of the
country. That assurance all now have; a man who will in this
manner dissolve an assembly constitutionally his superiors, then
prevent their meeting by armed force. . . .'[1] No admiration could,
for the young Bagehot, be too much for such a man. Only the
sobriety of Machiavelli is lacking. The Florentine secretary was
not amused by what he saw. 'Let it then be the prince's chief care
to maintain his authority; the means he employs, be what they
may, will, for this purpose, always appear honourable and meet
with applause; for the vulgar are ever caught by appearances and
judge only by the event.'[2] That is what Bagehot judged by,
precisely. Bagehot devotes a whole letter to the subject of the
morality of the *coup d'état*. The subject had a fascination for him.
He was, of course, a Utilitarian, and he applied his doctrine with
little enough subtlety. 'Mankind must be kept alive': therefore,
everything must be sacrificed to this end. There is a destructive
frivolity about his lumping together of 'Parliaments, liberty,
leading articles, essays, eloquence'[3] as things that must go by the
board to keep life going. It amounts to an assertion that, in comparison with the common comforts, all the rest is hot air. Bagehot
so explains the need for Napoleon's *coup*. 'According to the

[1] *ibid.*, p. 82.
[2] Niccolo Machiavelli, *The Prince*, Chapter XVIII (The translation is that of the
edition published by Philip Allan & Co., London 1925 (p. 111).)
[3] *Works*, I, p. 84.

common belief of common people, their common comforts were in considerable danger. The debasing torture of acute apprehension was eating into the crude pleasure of stupid lives.'[1] There is something singularly unpleasant about the tone of this, from someone who had had less cause than most for apprehension as where his next meal–to say nothing of his next respectful attentions–were coming from. Nor is the facility with which Bagehot gives approval to the government's severities, very agreeable. 'The severity with which the riot was put down on the first Thursday in December', he writes, 'has, I observe, produced an extreme effect in England. . . . But better one *émeute* now than many in May.'[2] He was presuming on his small experience. 'There are things more demoralising than death.'[3] It is the death of other people he is speaking of. It was not thus that Swift spoke of the sufferings of the lower orders. 'And when Esau came fainting from the Field, at the Point to die, it is no wonder that he sold his Birth-Right for a Mess of Pottage.'[4] There was no *saeva indignatio* about Bagehot; one might say there was, instead, an ugly frivolity. A few words of Swift sweep him away: 'When I am in Danger of bursting, I will go and whisper among the Reeds.'[5]

There is a good deal, in the third letter, about the national character and its influence on events. Some of it is in language which would no longer be tolerated. 'There are breeds in the animal man just as in the animal dog. When you hunt with greyhounds and course with beagles, then, and not till then, may you expect the inbred habits of a thousand years to pass away, that Hindoos can be free, or that Englishmen will be slaves.'[6] It became a strong point with Bagehot later that plenty of stupidity in politics was a good thing, and here we have the principle applied, stupidly enough for a politician, to the differences between the English and French. 'I need not say that, in real

---

[1] *ibid.*, I, p. 85. [2] *ibid.*, p. 86. [3] *ibid.*

[4] Swift, *Drapier's Letters, The Prose Works of Jonathan Swift*, edited by Herbert Davis, Basil Blackwell, Oxford, 1939–68, Vol. 10, p. 53.

[5] Swift, *op. cit.*, p. 115. [6] *Works*, I, p. 100

sound stupidity, the English are unrivalled.' And then, 'a French-man—a real Frenchman—can't be stupid.'[1] Bagehot evidently enjoyed a flashy success with such comments; he was, himself, always decidedly one of the suspect clever. It may be that his strategy was to bask in a reputation for cleverness when he was in business circles and, when he was in company where his wit was more likely to be challenged, to hold against his adversaries the superior wisdom of practical men.

The English Constitution is the work by which Bagehot is best known; it is, so to speak, the reason for Bagehot. Without that he would have been in the memory of economists as the author of a clever book on the money market and in that of general readers who browse in the second-hand shops as an essayist sensitive up to a point. The idea of his greatness—of his being, even, 'the greatest Victorian', rests on this book, for such an idea must rest on something. It has had other than literary supports. Not only have a lot of people read *The English Constitution* but influential people have had cause to remember it. Most classics are put out of mind, by most men of affairs, but one that purports to explain their own activities will not be lost sight of. A book which insinuates, as this one continuously does, that these activities are incomparably important and to be criticised by no standards but those of the actors themselves, is sure to be dear to them. And the actors are now very numerous, including all those lesser figures, who as journalists, officials, commentators or academics somehow contrive to make a living out of the conduct of the *res publica*. Bagehot's book has also the advantage of being readable, which is unusual in this class of literature, once the flutter of contemporary interest has gone. It is at any rate unusual, as Balfour pointed out, that a constitutional treatise can be re-garded as light reading. Bagehot's book is certainly that. It is

---

[1] *ibid.*, I, p. 101.

light, like so much of Bagehot's writing, with the style of a man who is letting you into a secret, or revealing something perfectly obvious which you, poor fool, have missed. Bagehot is not a very well-bred writer, and the herd of knowing commentators we now suffer from have a real affinity with him.

Descriptions of the Constitution, as Bagehot himself remarked, may exercise an immense influence. If the description is erroneous –which Bagehot naturally thought was the case with other people's descriptions–people may begin to act as if they were true. And indeed it is the nature of the subject that it is not easy to establish what is a true description. If one confines oneself to the legal forms in a state, it will no doubt be possible to say something reasonably accurate. Bagehot's claim, however, is to describe a reality behind the forms, which indeed he makes very light of. The bare legal forms certainly give an inadequate notion of the mechanism. Any constitution is custom as well as the more explicit proprieties. And custom–it may be, all behaviour–involves ideas, those enemies in practical affairs which Bagehot so derided. It is not enough to say, as Bagehot does in the *Letters on the Coup d'État*, that 'rigorous reasoning would not manage a parish vestry, much less a great nation'.[1] That is true, but it is not what is in question. Nor is it enough to speak of getting hold of 'some large principle'[2] as if it were merely the habit of some deluded people like the French. The human mind will produce reasons–often very sketchy ones–for its actions, and those reasons will be related to its conception–necessarily even sketchier–of reality as a whole. There is not even much hope, except provisionally and in a narrow field, of restricting the notions in play to a few of the kind that are called positive, based on ascertainable and confirmable fact. That is rarely possible even in those statistically supported memoranda which are so much used in the conduct of business, public and private, and which often conceal more intentions than they reveal. In discussing something so radical as an inherited constitution–and even the newest con-

---

[1] *ibid.*, I, p. 111.   [2] *ibid.*, p. 107.

stitution is based on inherited ideas—it is quite impossible. The whole body of our conceptions and preconceptions is involved. Bagehot conceived of his approach as being that of a reasonable man, and we know what an array of prejudices that figment may conceal. 'In discussing any Constitution,' he had said in looking at the one the French were currently giving themselves in 1851–2, 'there are two ideas first to be got rid of. The first is the idea of our barbarous ancestors—now happily banished from all civilised society but still prevailing,' he adds for the benefit of his liberal and Unitarian readers, 'in old manor-houses, rural parsonages, and other curious repositories of mouldering ignorance.' This is the notion that foreigners ought to have Kings, Lords and Commons like the rest of us. The second 'old idea' is 'that politics is simply a sub-division of immutable ethics.'[1] Of this misconception Bagehot gives a curious and rather revealing illustration—the idea that you have no more right to deprive a Dyak of his vote in a 'possible Polynesian Parliament, than you have to steal his mat'.[2] Politics was a field in which morals did not come into play, especially when all that was involved was the rights of Polynesians, Frenchmen, or perhaps more generally, the non-banking classes. Bagehot's description of the English Constitution, when he came to that, did not lack the colouring of his own preconceptions.

Indeed the *Letters on the Coup d'État* form an excellent preface to *The English Constitution* because they reveal Bagehot's ideas so nakedly. His sympathy for Napoleon le Petit was not superficial. 'Of course you understand,' he says, again in the tone he adopted when he was intending to astonish the Unitarians, 'that I am not holding up Louis Napoleon as a complete standard of ethical scrupulosity or disinterested devotedness.'[3] That is old Langport stuff, not to be regarded by a young man, however cautious, in Paris. But Louis Napoleon's 'whole nature is, and has been, absorbed in the task he has undertaken . . . he will coolly estimate his own position and that of France; he will observe all dangers

---

[1] *Works*, I, p. 97. [2] *ibid.* [3] *ibid.*, p. 86.

and compute all chances'.[1] He is indeed a man of business such as Thomas Bagehot would have approved. But of course he belongs to a wider world visible only to Walter–and to him, it might be said, only from a distance. How is a man like Louis Napoleon, 'by circumstances excluded from military and political life, and by birth from commercial pursuits, really and effectually to learn administration?' Not by reading Burke, Tacitus and Cicero. None of that old stuff! 'Yet take an analogous case. Suppose a man, shut out from trading life, is to qualify himself for the practical management of a counting-house. Do you fancy he will do it "by a judicious study of the principles of political economy" and by elaborately re-reading Adam Smith and John Mill?'[2] The 'analogous case' was precisely Bagehot's own, and the fancy he rejected was exactly his own method of preparation. But in this little fantasy Bagehot pours scorn on such notions. 'He had better be at Newmarket, and devote his *heures perdues* to the Oaks and the St. Leger. . . . Where too did Sir Robert Walpole learn business, or Charles Fox, or anybody in the eighteenth century?'[3] His ideal is that of the speculator. The shadow of Victorian morality has passed, to reveal the sunny smile of the successful gambler, though in practice Bagehot always hedged his bets with some caution. It is with regard to the fortunes of the winning classes that Bagehot sets out to examine the working of politics.

The famous distinction between the dignified and efficient parts of government is made at the very outset of *The English Constitution*. The dignified parts are 'those which excite and preserve the reverence of the population' and the efficient parts are 'those by which it, in fact, works and rules. There are two great objects which every constitution must attain to be successful . . . every constitution must first *gain* authority, and then *use* authority; it must first win the loyalty and confidence of mankind, and then employ that homage to the work of government.'[4] It is like a bank, in fact. It took the barges on the Parrett, the local

---

[1] *ibid.*, p. 87.   [2] *ibid.*, p. 88.   [3] *ibid.*   [4] *Works*, V, pp. 161-2.

reputation of Samuel Stuckey, the enterprise and London connections of Vincent, and the grave face of Thomas Bagehot, to
provide cover for the transactions on which Walter Bagehot
flourished; others had to be dignified so that the author of
Lombard Street could be clever. And it was the cleverness that
mattered. Bagehot was always preaching the merits of stupidity,
but he meant that smart-alecry could not survive without it. If
there is contempt, in Bagehot, for the 'inferior people', there is an
equal if more uneasy contempt for all that was above him. That is
why his book has so been taken up by the managerial classes; it
teaches admiration of themselves. Bagehot himself points out
that the two parts he describes in the constitution are not 'sep-
arable with microscopic accuracy'.[1] The Queen *could* be useful,
when she was helping the managers; a cabinet might even be
dignified, though this could not happen very often. The respect
for the higher powers was not respect *for* anything. Indeed the
only thing worth the respect of an intelligent man was what went
on inside the counting-house, but the vulgar would not understand that—better for them that they should not, perhaps. And the
efficient people were busied about being efficient; they were
above being respected except so far as there was something to be
got out of it. So loyalty had to find another peg, which would be
no more than a peg. It was no more than a confidence trick,
managed in the end by the banks. The matter was not put as
plainly as that. We have to wait for *The Monarchy*; Chapter I, in
the original edition, is *The Cabinet*.

Another preliminary sophism stands at the beginning of *The
English Constitution*. This is that there are classes of society which
correspond respectively to the states of development characteristic of various ages of history. 'We have in a great community
like England,' Bagehot says, 'crowds of people scarcely more
civilised than the majority of two thousand years ago; we have
others, even more numerous, such as the best people were a
thousand years since.'[2] He is wary of identifying these groups too

---

[1] *ibid.*, p. 161.   [2] *ibid.*, p. 163.

precisely with the social classes which were usually recognised. It is certain that his highest group is not meant to correspond with the highest social classes, though it is a well-placed group he has in mind. 'The lower orders, the middle orders, are still, when tried by what is the standard of the educated "ten thousand", narrow-minded, unintelligent, incurious.'[1] This is the sceptical *élite* who are at the core of Bagehot's social theory. The rest of the population are more or less contemptible. When Bagehot invites the reader to test his theory, it is with a remarkably narrow reference. While a member of the landowning or of the manufacturing classes might have suggested looking at the farmers and farm-labourers, or at the foremen and mill-hands, the banker's son can think only of going into the kitchen. 'Those who doubt should go out into their kitchens. Let an accomplished man try what seems to him most obvious, most certain, most palpable in intellectual matters, upon the housemaid and the footman, and he will find that what he says seems unintelligible, confused, and erroneous—that his audience think him mad and wild.'[2] One can imagine the servants at Herd's Hill: 'Mr. Walter do say some things.' His is not the voice of the country gentleman, speaking with respect of some special knowledge or skill among his retainers. The things he said were evidently not of the kind which struck his less sophisticated listeners as being on the bottom of reality. He was convinced of his superiority; he was less sure about what the lower classes had to offer. His social class, indeed, represents the beginning of that disjunction of management from which industry so notably suffers in our day. Bagehot was thorough-going about his theory of the retarded classes. 'Great communities are like great mountains—they have in them the primary, secondary, and tertiary strata of human progress; the characteristics of the lower regions resemble the life of old times rather than the present life of the higher regions.'[3] A certain time-lag in the diffusion of habits is, certainly, characteristic of the old, agricultural society. But Bagehot's theory of the co-

[1] *ibid.*   [2] *ibid.*   [3] *ibid.*

existence, in different classes, of the *mores* of different historical epochs goes much further than that. He is quite sure that all that does not belong to banking is appropriate to a more primitive age. 'The ruder sort of men—that is, men at *one* stage of rudeness—will sacrifice all they hope for, all they have, *themselves*, for what is called an idea—for some attraction which seems to transcend reality, which aspires to elevate men by an interest higher, deeper, wider than that of ordinary life.'[1] It is for this gullibility that the dignified parts of the constitution are designed, or at least preserved. One could hardly have a more complete identification of the dignitaries with religion and the ancestral voices, or a more complete dismissal of all such things as 'adjusted to the lowest orders—those likely to care least and judge worse about what *is* useful.'[2] The old dignitaries are, however, not entirely without relevance to the conduct of the better sort of men. Luckily such people are not inventive all the time, and the traditional parts of the constitution so to speak keep them together while they make their money. But the sole merit of the 'historical, complex, august, theatrical parts'[3] of the constitution, 'which it has inherited from a long past' is that it 'takes' the multitude, and the ten thousand intelligent people benignly go along with it. It is not only the ancient and dignified that 'takes' people and carries them along, however. The novel and undignified, of which Bagehot was the advocate, have an attraction scarcely less, and when, as in our day, the accepted ideas are those which lay claim to novelty and modernity, the 'carrying along' of people at large becomes a torrent. It is certainly not liberal ideas which lack apologists, in our day. Nor does anyone need to defend Bagehot's famous distinction between the 'dignified' and 'efficient' parts of government. It is regarded as self-evident, the truth itself. 'We have in England an elective first magistrate as truly as the Americans have an elective first magistrate. The Queen is only at the head of the dignified part of the constitution. The prime minister is at the head of the efficient part.'[4] This is doctrine children take

---

[1] *ibid.*, p. 164.   [2] *ibid.*, p. 165.   [3] *ibid.*, p. 166.   [4] *ibid.*, p. 167.

in with their mother's milk. It is a new separation of powers, only one of the two is not a power at all, but a sort of consumer luxury. Bagehot of course would not admit that. For him the merit of the monarchy is 'that it is an intelligible government. The mass of mankind understand it, and they hardly anywhere in the world understand any other'.[1] It could hardly be said, however, in Bagehot's day, any more than in our own, that the idea of a committee–a cabinet–deciding things was beyond the understanding of a country which had watched the French Revolution and had itself had, more than two hundred years before, a Long Parliament, and Standing Committees in every county expropriating and otherwise putting down all who inclined too much to the King's cause or indeed tried to use the Prayer Book. Bagehot did his best to make the notion of 'efficient' government sound difficult. Of course the details of any government will be boring and comparatively difficult but this has really nothing to do with the question whether people have wit enough to understand that the Queen is unimportant, and the cabinet important. 'The nature of a constitution, the action of an assembly, the play of parties, the unseen formation of a guiding opinion, are complex facts, difficult to know, and easy to mistake. But the action of a single will, the fiat of a single mind, are easy ideas: anybody can make them out, and no one can ever forget them. When you put before the mass of mankind the question, "Will you be governed by a king, or will you be governed by a constitution?" the inquiry comes out thus–"Will you be governed in a way you understand, or will you be governed in a way you do not understand?" '[2] Bagehot makes it sound very pat, but the illustration that follows shows the absurdity of what he is saying. 'The issue was put to the French people; they were asked, "Will you be governed by Louis Napoleon, or will you be governed by an assembly?" The French people said, "We will be governed by the one man we can imagine, and not by the many people we cannot imagine." '[3] But in fact not so many years before they had beheaded 'the one

---

[1] *ibid.*, p. 182.   [2] *ibid.*, p. 183.   [3] *ibid.*

man they could imagine' and run through a series of democratic devices until they settled on Napoleon I, not because they found assemblies unintelligible but because Napoleon had settled on *them* and because he was *efficient*, in the way the assemblies were not, as well as having, perhaps, his own style of dignity. Indeed the notion of separating the efficient and dignified parts of government is very corrosive. It is a way of discrediting part of the apparatus, and when people seek to discredit a bit of the machinery of government one should ask who they are and what they design to put in its place. There should be no doubt that, so far as the monarchy is concerned, Bagehot's book is intentionally subversive, and that, so far as his description of it is correct, he is describing a decayed polity.

The insistence, in *The English Constitution*, that the monarchy is merely a trick which clever men of affairs play off against the common people, is repeated. It is a symptom of Bagehot's contempt for those below him as well as for any who might be presumed to be above him. He is the middle-class man who *looks after himself*; he had not even children to deflect him from his complacent self-admiration, or to spill his resources. The 'labourers of Somerset' have a special disapproval reserved for them. Their sincerity when they touched their fore-locks was perhaps not all that he might hope for and even the pre-1867 voters of Bridgwater–themselves an *élite*–had refused to return him to Parliament. The Greek legislator, fortunate enough to have 'slaves to keep down by terrors', 'had not to deal with a community in which primitive barbarism lay as a recognised basis to acquired civilisation. *We have*,' he said, 'We have whole classes unable to comprehend the idea of a constitution–unable to feel the least attachment to impersonal laws.'[1] There is a prim shockedness about this, a horror of this race which knows about hedging and rabbitting and cider but does not care about the clever gentlemen who read the *Economist*. Yet Bagehot certainly did not wish to rouse these people to any too acute sense of their

[1] *ibid.*, p. 185.

political rights and he was against any reckless extension of the franchise, which might lead to the banking classes being under-represented, as he thought. The stupidity of the helots was really Bagehot's excuse for the monarchy. 'So long as the human heart is strong and the reason weak, royalty will be strong because it appeals to diffused feeling, and Republics weak because they appeal to the understanding.'[1] *Mutatis mutandis*, this might be an extract from one of the Sunday morning sermons preached by Thomas Bagehot in the drawing-room at Herd's Hill, on the rationality of Unitarianism and the mysteries practised in the church on the hill opposite.

Bagehot indeed goes on from these generalities to discuss the relationship of the monarchy with religion in a manner which shows little sympathy with either. What he gives us is a rather shoddy version of Whig history. A superstition of sanctity, holding up the march of constitutional progress, is all that re-mains of the other side of the argument. 'In former times, when our constitution was incomplete'–this 'incomplete' must have been inadvertent from one who believed that his subject was 'in constant change'[2]–'this notion of local holiness in one part' of the constitution, namely in the Crown, 'was mischievous. All parts were struggling, and it was necessary'–there is another kind of mystification here, that of the Progressive–'that each should have its full growth. But superstition said that one should grow where it would, and no other part should grow without its leave. The whole cavalier party said it was their duty to obey the king, whatever the king did. There was to be "passive obedience" to him, and there was no religious obedience due to anyone else. He was the "Lord's anointed", and no one else had been anointed at all.' How unfair that was! 'The Parliament, the laws, the press were human institutions; but the monarchy was a Divine insti-tution. An undue advantage was given to a part of the con-stitution, and therefore the progress of the whole was stayed.'[3] It is remarkable how much is jettisoned, in this argument. It is

---

[1] *ibid.*, p. 186.   [2] *ibid.*, p. 116.   [3] *ibid.*, p. 187.

not only the comedy of Bagehot's regret that the press, which after all had at this time hardly been invested with its later beatitude, had not been 'anointed' as the King in fact had been. The solid, one might say incontestable, legal argument that the 'parliament' had no authority to legislate without the king, and that the 'laws' were in fact not laws without him, is thrown aside. This is indeed the crux of Bagehot's method of description. There is no objective, legal situation to be explored. That sort of reasoning, which might allow of legitimate differences of opinion and even of rational solutions, is discarded. The great, objective *res publica* is pushed aside to enable the critic to start from his own prejudices. The 'diffused feeling' of the traditional Whig is where Bagehot starts from, and the pretensions of law and religion are ignored because 'they appeal to the understanding'.

Bagehot follows the Whig course of history in some detail, making great fun of the fact that the legitimate succession was deflected, to a greater or less extent, in William III, in Anne, and the Georges. It was as if all this had not been argued out, in principle, by Filmer and his critics. It is still supposed, in some quarters, to be extremely funny that Filmer derived all monarchy from Adam. He was not, however, such a fool as is sometimes made out. It is evident enough that crowns and thrones have been upturned, and that this did not happen for the first time in English history with William III. There is a vestige of the patriarchal notion in monarchy, and that our political notions should have a link with our more intimate psychology is not necessarily absurd. 'A *family* on the throne is an interesting idea also', as Bagehot said. For him it was interesting because 'it brings down the pride of sovereignty to the level of petty life'.[1] Another way of saying this would be that it ties monarchy to something more interesting, for the mass of mankind, than the doings of politicians and the leaders in the *Economist*. Bagehot is determined in his rejection of anything which resembles an incarnation. He is so highly evolved, in the direction of economics and banking,

[1] *ibid.*, p. 186.

that certain modes of thought escape him altogether. 'The nation is divided into parties, but the Crown is of no party. Its apparent separation from business is that which removes it both from enmities and from desecration, which preserves its mystery, which enables it to combine the affection of conflicting parties–to be a visible symbol of unity to those still so imperfectly educated as to need a symbol.'[1] This idea that superior men think wholly in abstractions–symptomatic of the turn of mind which accounts for the drift, in Bagehot's career as a writer, away from literature and towards business–is connected with his emphatic disjunction from the primitive, and more generally from everything which does not bear the mark of urban, and preferably banking, civilisation. The artist, and indeed the orthodox Christian, cannot fail to find in himself a kinship with primitive peoples, or to regard the accidents of the last few thousand years as making small difference in the essential nature of man. Faced with the caveman's drawings, or the crafts of some tribe surviving from the Stone Age, his attitude will be one of awed deference. Not so with Bagehot. 'If we look back to the early ages of mankind, such as we seem in the faint distance to see them–if we call up the image of those dismal tribes in lake villages, or on wretched beaches–scarcely equal to the commonest material needs, cutting down trees slowly and painfully with stone tools, hardly resisting the attack of huge, fierce animals–without culture, without leisure, without poetry, almost without thought'–he might have said, without drawing-rooms–'destitute of morality, with only a sort of magic for religion; and if we compare that imagined life with the actual life of Europe now, we are overwhelmed at the wide contrast–we can scarcely conceive ourselves to be of the same race as those in the far distance.'[2]

It is only after a whole chapter on the dignity of the Queen that Bagehot turns to the work she actually does. At the outset of this part of his study he exposes 'two errors' in 'the popular theory of the English Constitution'. The first is that the sovereign is 'an

[1] ibid., p. 191.   [2] ibid., pp. 162–3.

"Estate of the Realm", a separate co-ordinate authority with the House of Lords and the House of Commons'.[1] In the tone of supercilious patronage which is really Bagehot's main contribution to the theory of the monarchy, he says that the Queen 'must sign her own death-warrant if the two Houses unanimously send it up to her'.[2]

It is to be doubted whether the Whiggery of the English at large even now goes as far as that. Bagehot's argument is, of course, that because the Royal Assent to parliamentary bills is automatic, the idea that she has any legislative power belongs to the past. But this is not so. Acts of Parliament are still, without doubt, acts of the Queen in Parliament. With the complexity of modern government, and its dependence on consultation and opinion, it would obviously be folly for her to press her opinion, on a particular measure, and an attempt to do so, in normal circumstances, would lead immediately to a constitutional crisis which the ruling party of the day would almost certainly win. Consider, however, the situation which might occur in war and might indeed, had things gone worse for us, well have occurred in the war of 1939–45, in which rival 'governments' are established. There could be no doubt that the legitimate government would be the one whose advice the Queen took. It is equally certain that so-called Acts of Parliament made without her assent would have no more force than opinion cared to attribute to them. They would certainly not be the law of the land. Nor, at any other time, would a piece of paper which had not, in due form, received the Royal Assent, be an Act of Parliament which could be recognised in the courts. In asserting baldly that the Queen has no legislative power Bagehot is 'trying what seems to him most obvious, most certain, and most palpable in intellectual matters, upon the housemaid and the footman'.[3] One may be unpersuaded as they seem to have been at Herd's Hill.

The second 'error' which Bagehot exposes is 'that the Queen is the executive'.[4] He is afraid that people may not have noticed

---

[1] *ibid.*, p. 199.   [2] *ibid.*   [3] *ibid.*, p. 163.   [4] *ibid.*, p. 199.

the Prime Minister. It is evident that the Queen is not the equiva-
lent of the American president–a point on which he finds it
necessary to insist–and that many of the functions of the latter
are analogous to those performed by our Prime Minister. The
Queen is a passive head; she is also a permanent one. The Prime
Minister is active and impermanent; his impermanence is the
price of his activity. Bagehot is right in saying that 'in most cases
the greatest wisdom of a constitutional king would show itself
in well considered inaction'.[1] In the complexity of a modern
administration it could hardly be otherwise, and what is called a
decision, at any level in any organisation, is more often than not
nothing but a recognition of the facts. Bagehot cannot concede
the good sense of Queen Victoria and Prince Albert without some
gratuitous remarks about the abilities and education of princes.
It is evident that no hereditary system can guarantee a succession
of outstanding men, and that any such system should be so
devised as to make allowances for this. Bagehot however feels
bound to assert not only that 'the education of a prince can be
but a poor education' but even that 'a royal family will generally
have less ability than other families'.[2]

Once more one feels on the side of the footman who thought
his talk 'mad and wild'. In spite of the disparagements he utters,
Bagehot goes on to say that he thinks 'it may be shown that the
post of sovereign over an intelligent and political people under a
constitutional monarchy is the post which a wise man would
choose above any other'.[3] One cannot but feel that he has his eye
on the job. It is thwarting–and many editors seem to feel it–to
go on year after year commenting on public affairs without being
sure that anyone is listening to you. The English people, we have
seen, were in Bagehot's view far from being wholly 'intelligent
and political'. They were not all fitted to read the *Economist*, by a
long way. The job of a constitutional monarch in this country
could not therefore be all agreeable discussion, like theology.[4]
It was, however, the job in which the wise man–and certainly

[1] *ibid.*, p. 209.   [2] *ibid.*   [3] *ibid.*, p. 211.   [4] v. *supra*, p. 16.

Bagehot is thinking of himself–'would find the intellectual impulses best stimulated and the worst intellectual impulses best controlled'.[1]

Bagehot's evident inclination–if only his circumstances had been more favourable–towards seeking a post as a constitutional monarch, and more particularly the reasons he gives for his choice, are eminently characteristic of him. He was a man who liked to amuse himself, in a prudent way. He does not think of a job in terms of what he could produce in it; he is a member of the banking and not of the producing classes. He is a dilettante and not an artist or a man of action. He thinks of the job in subjective terms. He would be king in order to enjoy a flutter of intellectual impulses, rather as Walter Pater fancied getting a little 'high' on the drugs of art. His 'best' intellectual impulses were to be stimulated; there is no direct indication which they were, but one may guess from the indications he gives about the 'worst'. The worst were those which would be checked by a knowledgeable Prime Minister who had done the work and knew the facts, and so prevent King Walter making a fool of himself. Perhaps this distinction carries some recollection of occasions when his exuberance as a leader-writer had got ahead of the facts, and he had felt a little foolish afterwards. It would certainly be a bad impulse that made a fool of Walter Bagehot.

'To state the matter shortly,' Bagehot goes on, 'the sovereign has, under a constitutional monarchy such as ours, three rights– the right to be consulted, the right to encourage, the right to warn. And a king of great sense and sagacity'–this is Bagehot himself, and this is why he changes the sex of the sovereign–'would want no others. He would find that his having no others would enable him to use these with singular effect. He would say to his minister: "The responsibility of these measures is upon you. Whatever you think best must be done. Whatever you think best shall have my full and effectual support. *But* you will observe that for this reason and that reason what you propose is bad; for this reason

---

[1] *Works*, V, p. 211.

and that reason what you do not propose is better. I do not oppose, it is my duty not to oppose; but observe that I *warn*." Supposing the king to be right, and to have what kings often have'–a slip-up surely this, for he is talking of a poorly-educated class, from families with less ability than other families–'the gift of effectual expression, he could not help moving his minister. He might not always turn his course, but he would always trouble his mind.'[1] This is, no doubt, to some extent, the voice of experience. Bagehot, in a state of semi-detachment from the bank in order to pursue his journalistic interests, must often have treated his trembling managers to much this sort of discourse, *mutatis mutandis*. He goes on to liken the position of the constitutional monarch–and there is some truth in the comparison–to that of the permanent official who can warn and advise his minister from long-standing knowledge. He also points out the difference. The minister is the permanent official's superior–and no one who has watched the process would be disposed to deny that the relationship often deflects the course of the advice, in an official at once weak and ambitious–while in the sovereign the minister has 'to answer the arguments of a superior to whom he has himself to be respectful'.[2] There is nothing except the ordinary politenesses of conversation, and the need for tact in handling his man, to induce the sovereign to conceal his opinions. Bagehot fairly comments that permanence gives the king 'the opportunity of acquiring a consecutive knowledge of complex transactions, but it gives only an opportunity. The king must use it. There is no royal road to political affairs: their detail is vast, disagreeable, complicated and miscellaneous. A king, to be the equal of his ministers in discussion, must work as they work; he must be a man of business as they are men of business. . . . An ordinary idle king on a constitutional throne will leave no mark on his time; he will do little good and as little harm.'[3] Rather less fairly or at least less certainly, Bagehot follows this comment with another: '*corruptio optimi pessima*. The most evil case of the royal form is far

---

[1] *ibid.*, p. 212.   [2] *ibid.*, p. 213.   [3] *ibid.*, pp. 219–20.

worse than the most evil case of the unroyal.'[1] The evil case is of the meddling or corrupt constitutional monarch. But the worst case of the non-royal form is probably something different in kind—the passions roused by popular selection and the uncertainty of the succession from which monarchy is a protection. When he goes on to discuss the House of Lords, Bagehot reverts to the notion of *dignity* of which he had made so much in relation to the Crown, and of which in his day peers still had some. Once more he deplores the 'incredibly weak' fancy of the mass of men, which needs a visible symbol, and what he says has perhaps a touch of personal recollection about it. 'A common clever man'—though Bagehot was certainly never exactly that—'who goes into a country place will get no reverence; but the "old squire" will get reverence.' There is surely a touch of personal indignation here. Though Mr. Bagehot's clever son got some respect, no doubt he will have had less than the stupid landowners. 'Even after he is insolvent', he goes on revealingly, 'when everyone knows his ruin is but a question of time' —when the bank is going to close on him, in short—'he will get five times as much respect from the peasantry as the newly-made rich man who sits beside him.'[2] Really it is most unfair. Ah, the 'coarse, dull, contracted multitude, who could neither appreciate or perceive any other'[3] form of distinction, and did not care whether the bank got its money. But the banker is, after all, just as visible to the simple clown, or to anyone else, as the genuine squire, so that it cannot be visibility alone that determines who is taken as a symbol by the populace.

Bagehot has, however, some sobering things to say about the uses of a nobility—in his day, for in ours of course family is something to apologise for. A nobility 'prevents the rule of wealth'—for Bagehot is far too subtle to recommend that. The merely rich had to defer to traditional society. 'As the world has gone, manner has been half-hereditary in certain castes, and manner is one of the fine arts. It is the *style* of society; it is in the daily-spoken

---

[1] *ibid*, p. 220.   [2] *ibid.*, p. 222.   [3] *ibid.*

intercourse of human beings what the art of literary expression is in their occasional written intercourse.' One is almost in the world of Madame de Sévigné. 'In reverencing wealth we reverence not a man, but an appendix to a man; in reverencing inherited nobility, we reverence the probable possession of a great faculty–the faculty of bringing out what is in one.'[1] The tone is striking, after the incivilities to the Royal Family. It may be that Bagehot, on the fringes of public life, was prepared to be benevolent to the aristocracy for the sake of being preserved from the 'third idolatry'. This was perhaps the 'worst of any', the idolatry of office. 'In France and all the best of the Continent it rules like a superstition. It is to no purpose that you prove that the pay of petty officials is smaller than mercantile pay; that their work is more monotonous than mercantile work; that their mind is less useful and their life more tame. They are still thought to be greater and better. They are *décorés*, they have a little red on the left breast of their coat, and no argument will answer that. In England, by the odd course of our society, what a theorist would desire has in fact turned up. The great offices, whether permanent or parliamentary, which require mind now give social prestige, and almost only those. An Under Secretary of State with £2,000 a year is a much greater man than the director of a finance company with £5,000, and the country saves the difference. But except a few offices like the Treasury, which were once filled with aristocratic people'–and with which Bagehot had a sort of connection through his father-in-law, James Wilson, as well as, more remotely, through the early activities of his uncle Vincent Stuckey –'and have the odour of nobility at second-hand, minor place is of no social use.'[2] Bagehot had not attained office himself and he was glad to have the nobility to keep down the pride of those who were in office.

A good deal that Bagehot has to say about the working of the House of Lords was applicable in his day but is not in ours, for the House of Lords, that most fashionable of institutions, is

[1] *ibid.*, p. 223.   [2] *ibid.*, p. 224.

always changing. It is of general interest that he remarks that, even when the authority of the peerage was at its height–which was of course before Bagehot's day–the House 'was a second-rate force'.[1] This was because greatness of rank could not guarantee proficiency in the business of the House, and those who were proficient naturally took the lead. Before the Reform Act, however, the peers, with so much influence in the country, were able powerfully to influence the House of Commons, so that there were never two antagonistic chambers.

Nobody now supposes that it would do to have the two at odds. If the Lords in 1832 gave way because of the threat to create new peers, the House of Lords now has been so bludgeoned with threats of reform that it is in no doubt at all that its best defence against the more stupid of them is a reasonable concurrence with the House of Commons. As Bagehot says: 'With a perfect Lower House it is certain that an Upper House would be scarcely of any value. If we had an ideal House of Commons perfectly representing the nation, always moderate, never passionate, abounding in men of leisure, never omitting the slow and steady forms necessary for good consideration, it is certain that we should not need a higher chamber.'[2] It is far from certain that we are even now in that happy position.

As to what might be meant by representing the nation, Bagehot's ideas are not ours. He was writing before the Reform Act of 1867 when, according to Coventry Patmore, 'the false English Nobles and their Jew' were 'by God demented'[3] to the extent that they extended the franchise in the boroughs even to working-class householders. Bagehot was in favour of the erosion of the power of the Crown and of the land-owning nobility; he was not so extreme as to wish to see a similar fate overtake the banking classes. He saw that, in 1872, when he wrote the preface to the second edition of *The English Constitution*, it was still too soon 'to attempt to estimate the effect' of the 1867 Act, because the

---

[1] *ibid.*, p. 227.　　　　[2] *ibid.*, p. 235.
[3] Coventry Patmore, *Poems*, Bell, London, 1886, Vol. II, p. 289.

'people enfranchised did not yet know their own power'.[1] The difficulty of a long foresight did not prevent him, when he was writing his book in 1865–6, confidently foretelling the doom which various schemes of electoral reform then current would bring. 'The scheme to which the arguments of our demagogues distinctly tend, and the scheme to which the predilections of some most eminent philosophers cleave . . . would not only make parliamentary government work ill, but they would prevent it working at all; they would not render it bad, for they would make it impossible.'[2] The scheme favoured by the demagogues, 'the ultra-democratic theory', proposed nothing less than 'that every man of twenty-one years of age (if not every woman, too) should have an equal vote in electing Parliament'.[3] Under this preposterous arrangement, 'the rich and wise' were 'not to have, by explicit law, more votes than the poor and stupid.'[4] It is, certainly, very stupid to be poor and Bagehot, who had taken precautions enough, seems to have had a strong conviction that there is a close association between wisdom and riches. The second scheme, favoured by the philosophers (Mill is meant by this plural designation) was a form of proportional representation. It was an objection to a Parliament elected on manhood suffrage under the 'ultra-democratic scheme' that it 'could not be composed of moderate men' and if there were equal electoral districts, 'the scattered small towns which now send so many members to Parliament, would be lost in the clownish mass',[5] that is to say, would be swamped by the agricultural interest. Langport itself, as Bagehot liked to recount, had petitioned in the Middle Ages to be spared the expense of sending a member to Parliament. The objection to the philosophers' scheme is more interesting. It is that it would lead to 'the return of party men mainly'. This, to Bagehot, was highly objectionable. 'You would get together a set of members bound hard and fast with party bands and fetters, infinitely tighter than any members now.'[6] The voters would

[1] *Works*, V, p. 117.
[2] *ibid.*, pp. 262–3.
[3] *ibid.*, p. 263.
[4] *ibid.*
[5] *ibid.*
[6] *ibid.*, p. 268.

keep altogether too close a grip. 'The members,' he says, 'will be like the minister of a dissenting congregation. That congregation is collected by a unity of sentiment in doctrine A, and the preacher is to preach doctrine A; if he does not, he is dismissed. At present a member is free because the constituency is not in earnest: no constituency has an acute, accurate doctrinal creed in politics.'[1] Geography is a better basis for representation than principle. Against our sort of democracy Bagehot saw no protection except the monarchy, or rather the illusions which monarchy could produce in ignorant persons who had not read *The English Constitution*. 'The mass of uneducated men could not now in England be told "go to, choose your rulers,"; they would go wild; their imaginations would fancy unreal dangers, and the attempt at election would issue in some forcible usurpation. The incalculable advantage of august institutions in a free state is, that they prevent this collapse.'[2] But 'if you once permit the ignorant class to begin to rule you may bid farewell to deference for ever. Their demagogues will inculcate, their newspapers will recount, that the rule of the existing dynasty (the people) is better than the rule of the fallen dynasty (the aristocracy). A people very rarely hears two sides of a subject in which it is much interested; the popular organs take up the side which is acceptable, and none but the popular organs in fact reach the people. A people *never* hears censure of itself. No one will ever tell it that the educated minority whom it dethroned governed better or more wisely than it governs. A democracy will never, save after an awful catastrophe, return what has once been conceded to it, for to do so would be to admit an inferiority in itself, of which, except by some almost unbearable misfortune, it could never be convinced.'[3]

With *Physics and Politics* Bagehot moved on to the sort of essay in modern thought which such a man was sure to attempt some

---

[1] *ibid.*, pp. 269–70.   [2] *ibid.*, p. 341.   [3] *ibid.*, pp. 351–2.

time. The first part appeared in the *Fortnightly* in 1867, though the book did not come out until 1872. The sub-title is *Thoughts on the Application of the Principles of 'Natural Selection' and 'Inheritance' to Political Society*. It starts with the sort of invocation which has since become the stock-in-trade of popularisers: 'One peculiarity of this age is the sudden acquisition of much physical knowledge. There is scarcely a department of science or art which is the same, or at all the same, as it was fifty years ago. A new world of inventions.'[1] But it was, of course, Darwin above all on whom he was drawing for his new excitement. 'The problem is, why do men progress? And the answer suggested seems to be that they progress when they have a certain sufficient amount of variability in their nature.'[2] 'We need not take account,' he says elsewhere, a trifle exuberantly, 'of the mistaken ideas of unfit men and beaten races.'[3] The sentence shows how limiting, as well as liberating, may be the sudden sideways waft of the latest ideas from one science into another, or into a study which hopes to become another. With a flourish of Huxley's *Elementary Physiology* and Maudsley's *Physiology and Pathology of the Mind*, Bagehot lays down the dubious but to him clear proposition 'that there is a tendency, a probability, greater or less according to circumstances, but always considerable, that the descendants of cultivated parents will have, by born nervous organisation, a greater aptitude for cultivation than the descendants of such as are not cultivated; and that this tendency augments, in some enhanced ratio, for many generations.'[4] There is science for you. The book had a great success, but is very slight.

Taking his grand scientific look around the peoples of the earth, Bagehot sees war as making them into nations, customary law drilling them until they became genuine 'co-operative groups' and finally, in a few favoured cases, the 'age of discussion' liberating them and making progress possible. It is the modern world's view of itself. The servants and the peasants have dropped

[1] *Works*, VIII, p. 1.   [2] *ibid.*, p. 42.
[3] *ibid.*, p. 135.   [4] *ibid.*, p. 5–6.

from view. It may be thought that something else has dropped too. A 'progressive' view of society can hardly fail to place emphasis on the differences between one age and another to the point at which the similarities are almost lost from view. It is true that Bagehot says, in his most generalising vein, that 'unless you can make a strong co-operative bond, your society will be conquered and killed out by some other society which has such a bond' and that co-operation 'depends on a *felt union* of heart and spirit; and this is only felt when there is a great degree of real likeness in mind and feeling',[1] but he is thinking mainly of an earlier stage than that of the fully fashioned industrial society. He is thinking of the stage at which societies are formed by 'the most terrible tyrannies ever known among men–the authority of "customary law" '.[2] And he notes that this process goes on 'far away from all distraction'. 'All great nations have been prepared in privacy and in secret.' So it was with Greece, Rome, Judaea, which 'were framed each by itself, and the antipathy of each to men of different race and different speech is one of their most marked peculiarities'.[3] In this horrible condition 'trade is bad because it prevents the separation of nations'.[4] Bagehot hardly faced the implications of this for modern societies. Does it mean that, despite all 'progress', they are in inevitable decay? Perhaps he found a consolation, cynical enough, in the passion all societies have for uniformity. 'A new *model* of character is created for the nation; those characters which resemble it are encouraged and multiplied; those contrasted with it are persecuted and made fewer. In a generation or two, the look of the nation becomes quite different.' Those distressing squires and peasants give place to the more enlightened characters on Herd's Hill. 'A lazy nation may be changed into an industrious, a rich into a poor, a religious into a profane, as if by magic, if any single cause, though slight, or any combination of causes, however subtle, is strong enough to change the favourite and detested types of character.'[5] But if he applied this to contemporary industrial societies, he certainly failed to show how

[1] *ibid.*, p. 138.   [2] *ibid.*   [3] *ibid.*, p. 139   [4] *ibid.*   [5] *ibid.*, p. 133.

this ever-renascent conservatism could prevent them from sinking rapidly into the 'mummy-like' condition he scorned in societies still subject to customary law. 'It was "government by discussion" which broke the bond of ages and set free the originality of mankind.'[1] But there can be no doubt that such discussion tends to be conducted within a circle of prejudice which is itself limiting. Bagehot himself had, in *The English Constitution*, something to say about the unwillingness of democracy to hear any ill of itself.[2] In his delight at the passing of an order which demanded a certain subordination of himself he forgot this. 'Once effectually submit a subject to that ordeal'–discussion–'and you can never withdraw it again; you can never clothe it with mystery, or fence it by consecration; it remains forever open to free choice and exposed to profane deliberation.'[3] It does not, however, and the question remains what is to be a mystery, and what is the nature of the consecration.

Bagehot of course had answered that question. He had chosen one of 'the better religions' which 'have a great physical advantage'.[4] Truncating a problem which he could not solve, as he said, adopting a phrase of Sir William Hamilton, he opted for 'verifiable progress', 'that is, progress which ninety-nine hundreths or more of mankind will admit to be such, against which there is no established or organised opposition creed, and the objectors to which, essentially varying in opinion among themselves, and believing one thing and another the reverse, may be safely and altogether rejected'.[5] Obviously opponents of that model were to be 'persecuted and made fewer'[6] without mercy, so far as Bagehot was concerned. The model was provided by 'the plainer and agreed-on superiorities of the Englishman'[7] as he then was. It was 'the development of human comfort'.[8] With such a religion, many fripperies could be put aside.

---

[1] *ibid.*, p. 142.   [2] v. *supra*, p. 81   [3] *Works* viii p. 104.
[4] *ibid.*, p. 140   [5] *ibid.*, p. 134.   [6] v. *supra*, p. 83.
[7] *Works*, VIII, p. 135.   [8] *ibid.*, p. 144.

CHAPTER FOUR

The Art of Money

Having misdirected his youth towards the study of literature, for which he had no talent, and then towards the study of politics, to which he made a destructive contribution, Bagehot turned in his later years to wholly serious matters. *Lombard Street*, begun in 1870 and finished in 1873, is a paean in praise of money. We have the authority of Keynes for saying that, as a contribution to economics, it is of no great account. Keynes noted that it was one book which, at the time he was writing,[1] every economics student could be counted on to have read; he attributed this distinction to the desire of teachers of economics to conceal from the young student the fact that the subject was, in reality, not so amusing as Bagehot made it out to be. Bagehot did not, however, pretend that his book was a work of theory. Indeed, he went out of his way to emphasise that it was a description of concrete realities, and that is why he gave it a local instead of an abstract title. It was a study of the men who made money in the city, written by one who had a close acquaintance with many of those who dominated that scene, and who was by heredity as well as experience in the heart of the money trade.

Bagehot was writing in the great bulge of Victorian prosperity, and was conscious of these advantages, if that is what they were. His tone is that of a man showing off his plush furniture for the benefit of less fortunate people. 'Everyone is aware, he says, 'that England is the greatest moneyed country in the world; every one admits that it has much more immediately disposable and ready

---

[1] In 1915. See J. M. Keynes, *loc. cit.*, pp. 369ff.

cash than any other country. But very few persons are aware *how much* greater the ready balance–the floating fund which can be lent to any one or for any purpose–is in England than it is anywhere else in the world.'[1] Money was economic power, and Bagehot never asked the critical question as to whether this unprecedented concentration was a good thing, or whether it was a proper use of the dignified parts of government, about which he had written so cynically in *The English Constitution*, to act as a screen for the *sub-rosa* activities of bankers.

There is an almost childish lack of moderation about Bagehot's approach to his subject. In what he blithely called 'the non-banking countries', including Germany and France, there was more cash out of the banks than there was in England. But the French people, notoriously, would not part with their money. The result, though he did not specify it, was that France remained a predominantly agricultural country–or a backward country, as Bagehot would have said–while England moved rapidly toward a state of swollen manufacture and over-population, with consequences which are still with us, for good or ill, while the rest of the world has tried with some success to catch up. The distinction of England at this time was that it had an abnormal–and, historically regarded, perhaps morbid–amount of borrowable money. The banker collected a great mass of other people's money, and the borrowers gathered round him because, as Bagehot accurately said, they 'knew or believed' he had it. With a million pounds you could think of building a railway; leave that sum in its constituent tens and hundreds and you had to be content with scattered horse or donkey-carts. These technological benefits came less from the ingenuity of engineers and craftsmen than from the seminal virtue of trusting bankers. The system had a democratic tendency, but one that did not go too far. It eroded the power of hereditary wealth, but it did not go so far as to recognise the voices of those whom bankers did not trust. This was the *via media*, the *optimum* as far as Bagehot was concerned.

[1] *Works*, VI, p. 12.

He admitted that the new men created by easy credit and a wave of the banker's wand were, as a class, less honest than those who depended on a continuity of trade, and so of reputation. He admitted also that the system produced inferior goods because it relied on mere saleability, which could be achieved by relative cheapness, without regard to quality. But 'these defects and others' were 'compensated by one great excellence. No country of great hereditary trade, no European country at least, was ever so little "sleepy" . . . as England.'[1] To prove the indubitable supremacy of that excellence Bagehot relied upon Darwin. The propensity to variation was 'the principle of progress'.[2]

What it really amounted to was that men like Thomas Bagehot and Vincent Stuckey, placed at a point of vantage in an un-suspecting country-side, collected together the money produced by agricultural persons, who had no political thoughts, and transmitted it by way of London to Manchester and such places where entrepreneurs could then afford to pay wages which, miserable as they might be, were enough to attract people from the country-side to the mills where the new manufactures were carried on. Lombard Street was the go-between between the 'quiet saving districts of the country and the active employing districts'.[3] Bagehot admired without reserve the prompt way in which money flew to the places where it could produce most interest for the banker. The amount of profit being made was the sole thing that interested him; the fact that what is profitable to a particular entrepreneur may, on a wider or longer view, be uneconomic or even destructive, did not detain him for an instant. He would no doubt have sneered cleverly at William Barnes's distinction[4] between real and commercial value. Barnes was a Dorchester schoolmaster, a poet and a philologist. He was also the son of a small farmer and had seen the peasantry despoiled by the saving that went on in 'the quiet districts'. Bagehot noticed the money that was made; Barnes noticed other things.

---

[1] *ibid.*, p. 16.　　　　　[2] *ibid.*　　　　[3] *ibid.*, p. 17.
[4] William Barnes, *Labour and Gold*, John Russell Smith, London 1859, p. 23.

The peculiarity of the English economy, at this time, was that trade was conducted predominantly on borrowed capital. 'There never was so much borrowed money collected in the world as is now collected in London.'[1] Nearly all of it could be asked for any day the owners pleased, and if they did, the whole structure would come tumbling down. The ratio of cash reserves to bank deposits was unprecedentedly low. The whole system, therefore, might be thought, by the bystander who did not trust bankers enough, to be unstable. Bagehot himself recalls the 'astounding instance of Overend, Gurney, and Co.'[2] whose credit was almost as good as that of the Bank of England, but who none the less in a few years lost everything. 'And these losses were made in a manner so reckless and so foolish, that one would think a child who had lent money in the city of London would have lent it better.'[3] No doubt Messrs. Overend and Gurney none the less wore what appeared to be grown-up bankers' faces as they went impressively to and fro in the City. Perhaps there is some reason to doubt the efficacy of a system in which production stops or goes at the whim of money-lenders.

At the centre of this system was the Bank of England, which was conducted on much the same principle as other banks and which most people, including experts, believed to be essentially the same sort of institution. In a sense it was. Merchants kept their reserves at one of the lesser banks, which in turn kept their reserves at the Bank of England. On the board of the Bank of England they wrangled about how much money they had to keep idle, and complained that their dividend was low because they had to keep more than other people. In a manner the whole credit of the country depended on this ordinary commercial board. The wheels of trade and manufacture could stop because of the folly or misjudgment of these ordinary city characters. Everyone fortunately trusted the Bank of England but Bagehot obviously did not think that this trust was particularly well-

---

[1] *Works*, VI, p. 20.   [3] *ibid.*
[2] *ibid.*, p. 21.

founded. It was indeed persisted in in the face of evidence, for on various occasions the Bank had almost or quite suspended payment, or had had to be helped out in some way. What really distinguished the Bank of England from other banks was that, in the last resort, the government was behind it. That does, indeed, make a difference, not merely to the bank but to the nature of credit and, one might have thought, the standing of bankers. The whole system Bagehot describes is based on the assumption that money-lending is a private game, played by discreet men who, for reasons financial and personal rather than economic and public, could at any time interfere with the operation of the economy and regularly did so. This raises the question, which Bagehot did not pursue, as to how far such men are, for their private devices, operating in secret what should be regarded merely as part of the delegated authority of the state.

Bagehot does not pursue his enquiries in this direction merely because he has considered the matter and is so sure of his answer. 'No such plan would answer in England'–no such plan, that is, even as state management of the Bank. Bagehot's view is that the country could very well have done without the degree of intervention represented by the setting up of the Bank of England and by its special position. But for that, there would be a group of rival banks at the centre of things, as there are rival manufacturing interests, and this multiplicity would have given a greater security. But credit cannot be invented and since people trust the Bank of England it has to be left recognizably as it is. The political parallel Bagehot draws is characteristic. It would be easy, he says, to 'map out a scheme of Government in which Queen Victoria could be dispensed with . . . we know that the House of Commons is the real sovereign', for of course we have read *The English Constitution*, 'any other sovereign is superfluous'.[1] But stupid people will trust the Queen. In the same way–not stupid but–shrewd men of business have confidence in things holding together round the Bank of England; better,

[1] *ibid.*, p. 51.

therefore, leave it as it is. The whole plan of having political nominees 'would seem to an Englishman of business palpably absurd; he would not consider it, he would not think it worth considering'.[1]

But Bagehot saw clearly that the government of the Bank of England was in fact a national function; he would have the Board of Directors turned from semi-trustees for the nation to real trustees, with a trust deed which made their responsibilities clear. The system he recommended was, really, that the country should be run by men of business looking towards a written republican constitution, in the trust deed of the bank, while the eyes of the common people were averted in the direction of the Crown, where there was no power but, for vulgar minds, much entertainment. The theory of *The English Constitution* is really the counterpart of the theory of *Lombard Street* and it is the latter which is at the centre of Bagehot's notions of government.

The development of banking as a sort of arcane government under the cover of the publicly admitted forms was a relatively recent affair. It takes a long time to establish public confidence in a form of government, and the most stable constitutions are those which are accepted rather than explained. The growth of deposit banking, recent and still local, involved a similar growth. The essence of deposit banking was 'that a very large number of persons agree to trust a very few persons, or some one person. Banking would not be a profitable trade,' Bagehot goes on to confide, 'if bankers were not a small number, and depositors in comparison an immense number'.[2] It was of course part of the mystique of this shadow republic, growing up within the ludicrous monarchy of Queen Victoria, that you could trust it more than you could trust the government. It was supposed to represent the private interest of the depositor, though like all government it in fact involved releasing little atoms of private power to a more remote authority. The authority in this case was not the *res publica*, confused and uncontrollable but at least in

[1] *ibid.*, p. 53.   [2] *ibid.*, p. 56.

principle influenceable and subject to constitutional rules, but the mutual confidence of men in the city of London, some of the gravest of whom might on occasion behave like children, and who had no habit of responding to public criticism. The best way of encouraging the habit of deposit banking, Bagehot says, no doubt not unmindful of the affairs of the Somerset Bank and of Uncle Vincent, was 'to allow the banker to issue bank-notes of a small amount that can supersede the metal currency'.[1] This amounted to a subsidy to each banker–from whom he does not say–to keep the banker going until people, impressed by this mysterious power which makes money out of nothing, come along bringing their deposits, real money to take the place of the money the banker was in the first place allowed to imagine. One can quite see the desirability of keeping this arcane privilege to a few persons. Bagehot's account of this process is that of an acute and interested observer. The reason for its success is that, in the first instance, the initiative is entirely with the banker. All he requires is a public docile enough to do nothing but take his money and pass it from hand to hand. If people do not call his bluff by presenting the notes for payment, all is well. In time people begin to acquire piles of these notes. This makes them think what a trustworthy character the banker is, so they take along to him, and put on deposit, not merely his own notes but good coin as well. By preserving a grave exterior the banker has made money. One can understand the immense number of failures among early bankers, and the look of morality on the faces of those that survived. It is this conjuror's smile that we see again and again on the face of Walter Bagehot. He inherited it.

Bagehot recounts the history of the origin of the Bank of England, which his favourite Macaulay had told in a manner so suited to the exuberance of the age. Here was a Whig finance company, set up on the principle that while a Whig government was best for the city, even with such a government it was better for city men to trust themselves than the government. The city

[1] *ibid.*, p. 60.

would give countenance to the government rather than the government to the city. It was a phenomenon of settled times. A large Whig debt having been established, it became impossible to recall the Stuarts because they might repudiate it. The money-lender's notion of his ultimate rights over government, which coloured so much of the city's relationship with government from that day onwards, derives from this situation. The essence of the Whig settlement was that the court should sue for the support of the city rather than the other way round. Bagehot is wholly of this tradition. 'Nothing can be truer in theory than the economical principle that banking is a trade and only a trade, and nothing can be more surely established by a larger experience than that a Government which interferes with any trade injures that trade. The best thing undeniably that a Government can do with the Money Market is to let it take care of itself.'[1] One could not have a more categorical demand for 'hands off' the city. Such a demand is, in effect, a demand for the subordination of government to the men who trust one another with money. The idea of the government keeping its own money belonged to the infancy of the world. Happy if government had never meddled with banking at all. But in England it had done so, and a marvellous system, which would have regulated itself entirely on the self-interest of moneyed men, was now driven to rely in some measure on public opinion. The natural voice of this opinion was the Chancellor of the Exchequer, so we had better try and get one that knew his business. But Bagehot clearly conceives the Chancellor's main duty as being so to arrange his affairs that the money market is not upset, and that the game of confidence which begins with the local banker deciding whom to favour, and ends with the international market, can be played uninterruptedly in accordance with its own rules devised, of course, primarily for the benefit of the players.

It might be supposed that the Bank of England 'has some peculiar power of fixing the value of money'.[2] Not so, however,

---

[1] ibid., p. 70.   [2] ibid., p. 77.

according to Bagehot. Other people follow the Bank of England in what they charge for money, but there is no compulsion about this. They are quite free to do otherwise; it only happens that the Bank holds more money than other people and that has a certain influence on events. In effect it fixes a price, and what other people have to decide is whether they will enter into competition with this giantess, and offer money more cheaply, or whether they will charge a little more. It would seem that their freedom of action is somewhat limited. Unless anyone has an immense store of money, he will obviously get tired of offering it cheaply before the Bank bothers to bring its own rate down. As for offering money at a price above the Bank's, that is unlikely to be very alluring to customers. The caprice of the Bank is important, therefore, though Bagehot explains how, through the operation of supply and demand, it all comes right in the end, so that the Bank's power is not permanent; it is only great and sudden. A small matter, he seems to imply, though it causes some inconveniences, for 'up to a certain point money is a necessity'.[1] It is not the necessity of buying bread that Bagehot has in mind, but the anxiety of the merchant to find money in order to make more. 'If money were all held by the owners of it, or by banks which did not pay interest for it'—if it were designed solely for such low purposes as the exchange of directly useable goods, in other words —'the value of money might not fail so fast. Money would in the market phrase, be "well held".' But in Lombard Street money is held mainly by people who are borrowers as well as lenders. They must keep up a constant juggling of borrowing and lending, trying to make sure that the balance of the transactions is in their favour. The final secret of the market is that it must be run to the bankers' own advantage. This vital interest depending on it, one naturally wants to see a certain steadiness in the Bank of England, so that the lesser usurers are able to keep up with it.

With these important issues at stake, it is hardly surprising that 'Lombard Street is often very dull, and sometimes very

[1] *ibid.*, p. 80.

excited'.[1] It is rather on the same principle that other professions seem always to be more excited about their own jokes and vendettas than about the earthquakes and famines of the world at large. As an immense credit rests on a relatively small cash reserve, events such as a threat of invasion or the failure of a harvest bring with them the more serious trouble of a panic among bankers. A sudden apprehension that they may be short of money casts a blight on the whole community. There are 'good' times and 'bad' times; those that are good for bankers are good for everybody, those that are bad for bankers are bad for everybody. Certainly these warlocks should be propitiated! The identity of interest between capital and labour is complete, for the latter cannot hope to eat if the former is unhappy. The manufacturer, that secondary capitalist who is the banker's direct client, does not, as you might think, produce goods so that they can be *used*; he produces them 'to be exchanged'[2] because this is the operation in which there is most scope for the money-lender. The brisker the rate of circulation, the more the scope for lending and borrowing. The harder the manufacturer can be pressed, by his debts, to get his goods moving, the better. A man who carves pieces of wood, and puts them on a shelf to grow dusty until someone happens to come along who thinks it worth while buying one, is no use at all to the banker. He wants a manufacturer whose primary concern is a return on his money, and who thinks he has completed his mission if he produces any trash which can be sold above its cost, and the more the better, so that he has always to borrow to expand and can spare a percentage for the banker in the process. A depression or a slowing down of the circulation of trade, can be caused by one of two great natural forces—a calamity to a particular industry, agriculture especially, which produces goods people want to eat even more than they want to exchange them—and a failure of credit, caused by head-aches and migraines suffered by men with money who, on account of some disappointment, no longer trust one

[1] *ibid.*, p. 82.   [2] *ibid.*, p. 83.

94

another as much as they did. The two great natural forces are not unconnected. The picture is of the soul of the banker agonising within the crude body of industry.

A flicker of historical recollection crosses Bagehot's mind at this point in the argument. 'In our common speculations,' he says, 'we do not enough remember that interest on money is a refined idea, and not a universal one.'[1] There are even now unenlightened countries–most of the world, indeed, Bagehot says, in his day–where people do not trust the process of letting out money at usury. The real progress in civilisation came when people found they could have safe investments. There is an optimum stage of credit, attained in the year 1871 and characterised in the *Economist* as follows: 'We are now trusting as many people as we ought to trust, and as yet there is no wild excess of misplaced confidence which would make us trust those whom we ought not to trust.'[2] These good times are times of rising prices–produced by cheap corn, which the *Economist* was founded to campaign for, and cheap money–and not very welcome to 'quiet people' of 'slightly-varying and fixed incomes', but then it is not such people that Bagehot wishes principally to consider. They are, after all, unlikely to have their minds sufficiently on the kind of money games which mark our society with its peculiar qualities. The people Bagehot admires are those who, when a long-continued period of low interest has given way, by processes he describes, to a high rate, feel a sudden excitement, 'work more than they should, and trade far above their means'.[3] These are 'the ablest and the cleverest'–the money-makers, in short, those who have a peculiar gift for seeing beyond the vulgar surface of physical objects to the magical numbers which lie beyond.

Bagehot goes on to examine the rôle of the Bank of England in the panic of 1866. The Bank conceived that it had a duty to support the banking community, and so paid out its reserves till it hurt. No legitimate request for help, backed by proper securities, was refused. The *Economist* was so exuberant in its praise

---

[1] *ibid.*, p. 86.   [2] *ibid.*, p. 97.   [3] *ibid.*, p. 101.

of these proceedings, and of what it took to be an admission by the Bank that Mr. Bagehot's analysis of its function was the correct one, that Hankey, one of the directors, characterised the article as containing 'the most mischievous doctrine ever broached in the monetary or banking world in this country, *viz*. that it is the proper function of the Bank of England to keep money available at all times to supply the demands of bankers who have rendered their own assets unavailable.'[1] And indeed one can see that, in the round of confidence tricks desiderated by Bagehot for the proper maintenance of credit, there might well be some harm in the flat assertion that the Bank of England would always pay out to the lesser bankers. No doubt he had seen exactly where the interest of the lesser bankers lay; he was moreover, a journalist, and his striking and simple doctrine looked well in the *Economist*. The passage between Hankey and the *Economist* characterises Bagehot's position as a writer on public affairs. On the one hand he was never tired of pointing out, to the merely intellectual world, the solid good sense of men of affairs, himself included. On the other, he was delighted to exhibit to men of affairs, engrossed in mere business, the superiority of intellectuals, once more including himself. It is a position which gave him a sort of personal invulnerability, so long as he twisted and turned quickly enough, but one cannot be entirely without misgivings about so slippery an Achilles, with no heel. Bagehot's own analysis of the ineptitude of men of affairs, in matters of theory, is admirable. 'The abstract thinking of the world is never to be expected from persons in high places; the administration of first-rate current transactions is a most engrossing business, and those charged with them are usually but little inclined to think on points of theory, even when such thinking most nearly concerns those transactions. No doubt when men's own fortunes are at stake, the instinct of the trader does somehow anticipate the conclusions of the closet. But a board has no instincts when it is not getting an income for its members, and when it is only discharging a duty of office.'[2]

---

[1] *ibid.*, p. 108.   [2] *ibid.*, p. 113.

Yet it is to these alarming characters, lurching as instinct directs them towards their private profit, that Bagehot assures us that the control of credit and the public fortunes can safely be left. And what of the commentator? If he intrudes remarks for their wit or general truth rather than for the appositeness to a particular practical situation, is he more than a public entertainer who bedevils further the problems of the men who, by virtue of their position, have to find solutions or at any rate next moves?

Still, Bagehot is, in spite of the temptations of journalism, something more than a mere commentator. He is a banker from the skin inwards, and the attraction of his work on financial matters is that it is that of a man who can actually talk, with some facility, about the operations which his ordinary colleagues, the ordinary sensible men of business, merely perform. *Lombard Street*, as Keynes says, 'is a piece of pamphleteering, levelled at the magnates of the City and designed to knock into their heads, for the guidance of future policy, two or three fundamental truths. . . . Perhaps the most striking and fundamental doctrine . . . is, in a sense, psychological rather than economic . . . the doctrine of the Reserve, and that the right way to stop a crisis is to lend freely'.[1] Psychologically, it might be added, the appeal of the doctrine to Bagehot was that he was recommending *other people* to lend freely, in time of panic, as a way of saving Bagehot. He describes the panic of the Money Market rather as one might have described the Fire of London, and indeed it must have been rather like that. The bad news would 'spread in an instant through all the Money Market at a moment of terror; no one can say exactly who carries it, but in half an hour it will be carried on all sides, and will intensify the terror everywhere'.[2] This was perhaps the central horror of his life, next to the madness of his mother.

Bagehot goes on to describe the government of the Bank of England, as it was in his day. The board was self-electing, and although in theory a certain number went out each year, it was

[1] J. M. Keynes, *loc. cit.*, pp. 371–2.   [2] *Works*, VI, p. 125.

always some of the younger ones who went, so that the real power lay in the hands of a collection of ripe old men. When they chose a new director they did so with scrupulous care–'purity', is the word Bagehot uses, and it had a certain meaning for him–because if he stayed he would, twenty years later, infallibly become in turn Deputy Governor and Governor, for those offices were filled by seniority. They came to all in turn, and those who had held office–'passed the Chair'–formed the Committee of Treasury which exercised the real power in the establishment. By custom, none of these directors was a banker, in the ordinary sense of the term; they were merchants coming from reputable city houses. No wonder they needed Stuckey's to lecture them on the principles of banking! Bagehot indeed had a revolutionary proposal. It was that, since the Bank did not have a permanent Governor, and moreover had no one but subordinates about the place who understood banking, they should employ a sort of Permanent Under Secretary, on the model of Whitehall, to run it. Such a man as Bagehot himself would have filled the bill entirely.

Lombard Street is, in many ways, the most personal of Bagehot's books. His heart lay not only in the money but in the game of confidence he had inherited from his father and uncle in Somerset. He saw that banking was changing, and, correctly, expected that private banking would come to an end. The paragraphs in which he celebrates the life of that *milieu*–his own–comes nearer to poetry than anything he ever wrote:

'I can imagine nothing better in theory or more successful in practice than private banks as they were in the beginning. A man of known wealth, known integrity, and known ability is largely entrusted with the money of his neighbours. The confidence is strictly personal. His neighbours know him, and trust him because they know him. They see daily his manner of life, and judge from it that their confidence is deserved. In rural districts, and in former times, it was difficult for a man to ruin himself except at the place in which he lived; for the most part he spent his money there, and speculated there if he speculated at all. Those who lived there also would soon see if he was acting in a manner to shake their confidence. Even in large cities, as cities then were, it was possible for most persons to ascertain with fair certainty the real position of conspicuous persons, and to learn all that was material in fixing their credit. Accordingly the bankers who for a long series of years passed successfully this strict and continual investigation, became very wealthy and very powerful.

'The name "London Banker" had especially a charmed value. He was supposed to represent, and often did represent, a certain union of pecuniary sagacity and educated refinement which was scarcely to be found in any other part of society. In a time when the trading classes were much ruder than they now are, many private bankers possessed a variety of knowledge and a delicacy of attainment which would even now be very rare. Such a position is indeed singularly favourable. The calling is hereditary; the credit of the bank descends from father to son: this inherited wealth soon brings inherited refinement. Banking is a watchful, but not a laborious trade. A banker, even in large business, can feel pretty sure that all his transactions are sound, and yet have much spare mind. A certain part of his time, and a considerable part of his thoughts, he can readily devote to other pursuits. And a London banker can also have the most intellectual society in the world if he chooses it. There has probably very rarely ever been so happy a position as that of a London private banker; and never perhaps a happier.'[1]

Lombard Street was finished in 1873. 1876 was the centenary of the publication of *The Wealth of Nations*. Bagehot wrote two essays on this occasion—or perhaps one should say an essay and an article, the latter for the *Economist*, the former, closely related and in points repetitive, for the *Fortnightly*. The contribution to the

[1] *ibid.*, pp. 164–5.

Fortnightly, Adam Smith as a Person, is perhaps Bagehot's best essay. He had a subject completely to his liking, and completely within his scope.

Adam Smith was a man Bagehot felt he could patronise. A man inferior to himself, and yet who had produced such notable results in the world: What might not then Bagehot himself produce? Smith was born in Kirkcaldy in 1723, in a world far enough off in time as in place from Bagehot's English province. 'He was never engaged in any sort of trade, and would probably never have made sixpence by any if he had been.'[1] This lack of practical experience, in a man who passed for the inventor of political economy, needed some explaining. He was an awkward, unplausible man in comparison with Bagehot. He had a scheme, typical of the more superficial side of the eighteenth century— the Whig-*encyclopédiste* side—for a vast work on the development of the human mind and of social laws, on everything, in short. He went at this with Scotch and professorial industry until the acquisition of a sinecure made all intellectual work impossible. He picked up and much elaborated the talk of Glasgow merchants, and spent three years in France as tutor to the Duke of Buccleuch and there, as Bagehot put it, observed the numerous 'errors, such as generally accompany a great Protective legislation'.[2] The administration of France, then as now, showed a certain weakness for logical complexity. Worse still was the tendency of this legislation. Bagehot says that 'her legislators for several generations had endeavoured to counteract the aim of nature'— which was to confine her to agriculture and so make room for the English trade—'and had tried to make her a manufacturing country and an exporter of her manufactures'.[3] Reasoning on all these matters was Quesnay, who had a place at Court and excited himself about *'acheter, c'est vendre'* while Madame de Pompadour ran the government downstairs. The frank admiration for competition, which would infallibly produce fair prices, made an impression on Adam Smith, whose academic mind was probably

---

[1] *Works*, VII, p. 1 (*E.* III, 85).   [2] *ibid.*, p. 18.   [3] *ibid.*, p. 17.

also not unsympathetic to the governmental fantasies of the *économistes* who had 'the natural wish of eager speculators, to have an irresistible despotism behind them and supporting them; and with the simplicity which marks so much of the political speculation of the eighteenth century, but which now seems so childlike,' says Bagehot, 'never seemed to think how they were to get their despot, or how they were to ensure that he should be on their side'.[1] The gruesome admiration of eighteenth-century intellectuals for such characters as Frederick the Great is no more comic than the delusions of those of the twentieth century who have imagined that a Communist government would do what they wanted. After his residence in France Adam Smith went back to Kircaldy and lived with his mother for six years. After this he spent three years in London, still thinking, and then *The Wealth of Nations* appeared.

There are some acute comments on Adam Smith's conception of political economy in Bagehot's *Economic Studies*. Bagehot points out that this aboriginal author 'never seems aware that he is dealing with what we should call an abstract science at all. *The Wealth of Nations* does not deal, as do our modern books, with a fictitious human being hypothetically simplified, but with the actual concrete men who live and move. It is concerned with Greeks and Romans, the nations of the middle ages, the Scotch and the English, and never diverges into the abstract world.'[2] On the other hand, because Adam Smith's mind was rather crabbed and limited, he thought people were far more rigorous in pursuit of gain than most of them in fact are. He mentions some of the other things that people get up to, but his description is one-sided. He does not abstract more than he can help, but his mind is really of a self-limiting and so abstracting kind. People think him very practical, as compared with modern economists, because he professes to deal with the whole of man, but they are impressed by him because he deals only with part. By contrast, Bagehot says, the modern economists who make a deliberate

[1] *ibid.*, p. 22.   [2] *ibid.*, pp. 176–7.

abstraction of the economic man, while really, he implies, understanding the whole range of human nature, strike people as mere theorists. This is an argument from which we can afford to stand aside, but it may be remarked that the simplicity of mind, which led Adam Smith to the Utopia of Free Trade, is not much complicated in his nineteenth-century successors who thought that nothing could go amiss if it were established without hindrance in their native land.

One can hardly do better, if one wants an impression of the exuberance of solid men, in Bagehot's own circle, on the subject of free trade, than look at the prospectus which formed the preliminary number of the *Economist* (August, 1843). The immediate object of the new 'political, commercial, agricultural and free-trade journal' was the abolition of the Corn Laws, on which liberal opinion had fixed with the blinkered tenacity with which it has seized, since that day, on a succession of high causes which, viewed historically, are no more than successive expressions of the growing appetite of industry. The argument of free trade was from the first a financial argument. In James Wilson's eloquent prospectus the actual trades and actions of men are made to disappear before our eyes–they are explicitly treated as nonexistent if they do not satisfy the financial conventions of the time. 'As long as railways and canals are profitable', he says, 'they truly represent in real wealth the capital invested; but diminish the amount of traffic only so much as pays the profit– . . . and they are no longer wealth.'[1] In these terms there was over-production, even at this early stage of mechanised industry, and 'There is no cure, there is no remedy, for all these evils but increased demand; there can be no increased demand without increased markets; and we cannot secure larger markets without an unrestricted power of exchange, and by this means add to our territory of land, as far as productive utility is concerned, the corn fields of Poland, Prussia, and above all, the rich and endless acres of the United States.'[2] There might well be some hesitation,

[1] *The Economist*, preliminary number and prospectus, August, 1843, p. 5.   [2] *ibid.*, p. 7.

less than a generation after the Napoleonic wars, about a system based on the accessibility of the fields of Prussia and Poland. Even if this were not so, one might wonder how, on this basis of territorially expanding markets, 'we might go on increasing our production without limits'.[1] The doctrine of free trade was, after all, no more than the mood which went with markets which were in fact then expanding. If it was, as for Wilson, 'this only natural state of things'[2], it was so for people who had rejected Hobbes's state of nature in favour of a more optimistic tradition.

Bagehot had an eye for the entertaining detail of Adam Smith's work–how long it took waggons to go from Edinburgh to London, how many apprentices a master cutler could have in Sheffield, or a master weaver in Norwich. But the subject of his essay is Adam Smith himself, and there is a sort of personal curiosity about the way he treats the events of his fellow-economist's life. The parallel is never exact–indeed there is hardly a parallel at all–but Bagehot is thinking of his own involvement in practical affairs when he makes play with Adam Smith's appointment, after the publication of *The Wealth of Nations*, as a commissioner of customs. Well acquainted with the theory of taxation, 'he could have given a Minister in the capital better advice than anyone else as to what taxes he should impose'.[3] Just like me! Bagehot no doubt thought; was he not 'the spare Chancellor'? On the other hand, Adam Smith's not very weighty duties prevented him from writing any more. A point of contrast with the banker of Langport! 'And not unnaturally, for those who have ever been used to give all their days to literary work, rarely seem able to do that work when they are even in a slight degree struck and knocked against the world.'[4] Bagehot puts on a brave face before the loss of his predecessor's works. He says, truly enough no doubt, that what was lost was probably not very valuable. So Adam Smith lived on for fifteen years after the publication of *The Wealth of Nations*, talking sense among the lawyers and professors of Edinburgh and saying, at the end, that he meant

---

[1] *ibid.*   [2] *ibid.*   [3] *Works*, VII, p. 27.   [4] *ibid.*, p. 28.

to have done more. His mind no doubt was still full of his great scheme, with which in the end he did not weary the world.

❧❧❧❧❧❧❧❧❧❧❧❧❧❧

Bagehot himself was, towards the end of his life, occupied with a great work which Hutton appeared to think he might be finishing off in heaven. It was an economic treatise, to be in three parts, the first of general economic theory, the second a critique of some classic theorists, and the third containing portraits of great economists. The essay on Adam Smith is clearly the prototype of the work which would have made up the third part. What Bagehot had done of the first and second parts became the posthumous *Economic Studies* (1879). This work is therefore of a fragmentary nature, but perhaps we put up with the loss of the rest of it as well as Bagehot put up with the loss of the work Adam Smith did not do because he was distracted by the Customs. Bagehot is an unsystematic writer and it is unlikely that his book would have been a landmark in economic theory.

The *Economic Studies* open with an essay which appeared in the *Fortnightly* in 1876 under the title of *The Postulates of English Political Economy*. The essay starts with a reference to Adam Smith and goes on to inquire why English political economy was not popular outside England. One reason he alleges is it was 'more opposed to the action of Government in all ways than most such theories. . . . All Governments', he says, 'like to interfere; it elevates their position to make out that they can cure the evils of mankind'[1]–a rôle which, in Bagehot's view of things, is rather that of bankers who, by the stimulation of trade through money-lending, produce comfort, which is what we most desire. Another reason was simply that political economy was 'the science of business' which at that time was held to be fully developed only in

[1] *ibid.*, p. 94.

this country, as nowadays it is held to be fully developed only in the United States. Although he used this phrase, Bagehot was hardly on the side of the 'scientists' in this field. He was sceptical of the excessive hope in numeracy which has now swept through the minds of experts in affairs like a blinding lunacy. He was convinced of the treachery of figures; he knew how 'the names remain, while the quality, the thing signified,' changed. 'Statistical tables, even those which are most elaborate and careful, are not substitutes for an actual cognisance of the facts: they do not, as a rule convey a just idea of the movements of a trade to persons not *in* the trade.'[1] Yet Bagehot was not on the side of mere non-statistical common sense either. He was superior to the academic student of business because he was *in* trade, and to the ordinary man of business because he was clever. He takes neither side of the argument very far and characteristically rests in a position where he feels that no-one can get at him. As a conclusive illustration he alleges that, 'extraordinary as it may seem, the regular changes in the sun have much to do with the regular recurrence of difficult times in the money market'.[2] It is a striking assertion, which perhaps goes to the root of Bagehot's religious faith.

The essay goes on to comment on two unfruitful methods of investigation, still in principle very popular. One is what he calls the 'all-case' method, which pretends to the impossible task of collecting all the facts before proceeding to a theory. This method Bagehot traces to Bacon's early fumblings after an empirical method. The other unfruitful method is what he calls the 'single case' method, which consists in an exhaustive analysis of a particular group of facts. Bagehot quite rightly holds that no exercise in the manipulation of facts can be useful without a preliminary theory. Even so, with a sense of the fluctuation of things which almost overwhelms any belief in the existence of man as an, historically speaking, relatively unchanging species, he sees political economy–English Political Economy, as he calls

[1] *ibid.*, p. 99.   [2] *ibid.*

it—as concerned only with a particular recent group of phenomena. 'It is the theory of commerce, as commerce tends more
and more to be when capital increases and competition grows.'[1]
He proceeds to examine the conceptions of the transferability of
labour and of capital in light of these limitations. He has no
difficulty in showing that there are many conditions of society in
which these conceptions do not hold. The revelation will cause
little astonishment to any reader who stands a little apart from the
Great Commerce in which Bagehot revelled, but Bagehot himself
certainly did not draw the full consequences from this glimpse of
the subjectivity of economic notions. His common insistence
on the superiority of common sense, and of the notions of practical
men, in business or politics, over those religious and political
ideas which have a longer grip on the mind, is shown to be mere
bravado, the valueless talk of a class of men who happen to be
fashionable with themselves at a particular moment of history.
Bagehot repeatedly claims that men of business, economists and
bankers are concerned with 'hard' fact, as if it were a special kind
of truth. It is simply the one he loves best. 'Now of course it is
true that there are some things, though not many things, more
important than money,' he said in his centenary article on *The
Wealth of Nations* in the *Economist*, 'and a nation may well be
called on to abandon the maxims which would produce most
money, for others which would promote some of these better
ends. The case is much like that of health in the body. There are
unquestionable circumstances in which a man may be called on to
endanger and to sacrifice his health at some call of duty. But for
all that bodily health is a most valuable thing, and the advice
of the physician as to the best way of keeping it is very much to
be heeded, and in the same way, though the wealth is occasionally
to be foregone, and the ordinary rules of industry abandoned,
yet still national wealth is in itself and in its connections a great
end, and economists who teach us to arrive at it are most useful.'[2]
The key to this passage is the equation of wealth with money, an

[1] *ibid.*, p. 108.   [2] *Works*, IX, pp. 199–200 (*E*. III, 113).

error which Adam Smith had sought to remove, and which Bagehot understood very well, only to forget it in his passion for the refinements of credit, of which he was a powerful and hereditary practitioner.

CHAPTER FIVE

Some Considerations

One very suspicious circumstance about the reputation of Walter Bagehot is that almost nobody has a word to say against him. Somehow the aura of admiration which surrounded him in his domestic life has remained. There is comedy in the ingenuous praise of Mrs. Russell Barrington. It is so much that of a nice lady, enthusing over the really nice man of the family. 'While Bagehot was at this time leading a stirring social and family life,' she writes of her hero at the time of the Second Reform Bill, 'and at the same time one of pressing business.' This is the buoyant character who breezes in from such important work and people, placing his hat and gloves on the hall-stand while the ladies, hearing his footstep, put aside their needle-work or their water-colours . . . 'while', she goes on, 'he was watching every public event at home or abroad'–like the men who talk in trains or the interminable army of commentators who broadcast perpetually about matters of which, after all, they can know nothing– 'weighing the rights and wrongs of every current question of importance and giving judgment thereon in the pages of *The Economist*'–ah!–'interviewing and advising statesmen respecting measures to be brought before Parliament'–a television man before his time, indeed–'a subtle machinery was at work in his brain.'[1] No doubt. But the quality and importance of the products of that machine can be variously estimated. It was a former editor of *The Times* who was chosen to write 'a literary appreciation' of Bagehot for the *Economist*'s edition of his works. A Member of

[1] Barrington, *Life*, p. 382.

Parliament and publicist was chosen to edit it. It was G. M. Young, 'this generation's undisputed guide to the Victorian age', as William Haley calls him,[1] who found that Bagehot was 'the wisest man of his generation'.[2] A well-placed trio to carry Mrs. Barrington's praises to their conclusion. There is a certain social tone about the Bagehot coterie. He comes to roost among the cocks on the middle perches, that Oxford middle class whose undue influence is only now coming to an end in the conclusions they have for several generations contrived for with varying degrees of wall-eyed percipience.

It is in this discreet class—typically of civil servants, dons, editors of the middle-brow organs of opinion—that Walter Bagehot has been plentifully re-incarnated. There have been thousands of him, and the phalanx is only now beginning to grow a little thin. G. M. Young caught a glimpse of his fellow-marchers, which is very creditable in him, for it is a peculiarity of this kind to emphasise their own individuality and differences. There 'are thousands of people thinking and even speaking Bagehot today', Haley quotes him as saying, 'who might be hard put to say when exactly he lived and what exactly he did.'[3] No wonder. The bright intelligent, well-informed, quietly well-off, quietly corrupt, sufficiently successful, mutually helpful, are much alike. But the succession to Bagehot is less a phalanx than a congeries of ideas, and less a congeries of ideas than a tactical attitude, the manifestations of which vary slightly with the *milieu*. Hutton noticed that Bagehot never remained long in untenable positions, and never returned to them. The secret of his attitude is that the position mattered less to him than the tenability. He was therefore a man bent on looking after himself—an economist of her person, as Smollett said of Ferdinand Count Fathom.

It cannot be denied that this is an eminent virtue in a man of affairs. In almost all professions, once a certain mediocrity of

[1] *E*, I, 84.
[2] G. M. Young, *Victorian England, Portrait of an Age*, 2nd ed., O.U.P., London, 1953.
[3] *E*, I, 84.

intelligence is passed, what matters is ability to live in the *milieu*. The public at large do not know a good doctor or solicitor from a bone-headed one; success goes to the one who has the *air* of being a doctor or solicitor, according to the canons of the time. Being right or wrong is rarely of any importance; the best men have their excuses even when they are most blatantly caught out. But generally they do not have the appearance of being caught out. The patient dies, or some inscrutable legal difficulty raises its head, or the knavery of somebody else springs into sudden prominence. No very searching objectivity haunts the ordinary occupations of the banker. No doubt in an extreme case his bank can fail, but normally one muddle will pay off another, and the important thing is to seem to be doing all right. These arts, we may be certain, Bagehot had in sufficient measure, in what is called practical life. All that, however, has gone the way of the bank-notes of the Somerset Bank. The question that remains is whether the tactical evasion, so useful in day-to-day business, makes a durable contribution in literature.

In a sense it may be said that it does. One cannot locate Shakespeare in a stateable position, and the many statements as to what he 'thought' serve only to emphasise that he is something more elusive. It would be the claim of Bagehot's admirers, perhaps his own claim, that it is the same sort of nakedness before reality which gives his books on government, or on the money market, their value. He does not carry theory very far, it might be said, because he sees the whole complexity of the real world, and presents that. Or it might be said that he is the 'practical' man, dealing with 'hard' facts. The dwarf is the same as the giant, and the country banker, rightly understood, operates in a way remarkably like Shakespeare's. Is there not a comparable freedom of mind? Neither cares for a principle, if it does not suit him. Neither can be nailed down. The practical man is an artist, everything he deals with is provisional. There is a difference, however. What the artist leaves is not provisional, and does not disappear with yesterday's overdraft. Shakespeare prostrated himself before reality, because he could not help it. The little man of affairs takes the bits he can use for some mean purpose he sees, and comes out on top.

Bagehot's distinction was to have carried this technique of affairs into the business of writing. He was a journalist. Nearly all his writing was done, in the first instance, for the periodical press. So was De Quincey's, but De Quincey was no mere success and all the time he was looking for a point of rest behind the confusions of the matters of the day. With Bagehot, the provisional became so far as is possible a principle. You had to move smartly to keep up with him. He used his observations not to define his position, for he had none, but to defend himself. His method was not to yield to reality but to be clever about it, and to ingratiate himself sufficiently to make sure that he was not left alone. There is an affable, matey tone about his work which has made thousands of mediocrities feel at home with him. He is not only clever himself, but gives a distinct impression that he is one of a band of like-minded conspirators, to which the reader is invited to attach himself. This accounts for the destructive element in much of his work.

It is a trick which has often passed for liberalism. Bagehot's account of *The English Constitution* is based on it. Everything which has claims to be objectively important is smilingly shown to be unimportant, or important in some arcane way intelligible only to the group of conspirators, who will never submit to any truth unless it is manifestly useable to their own advantage. The plausibility of this position lies in the fact that, precisely, it is advantageous to know the truth. The real question is as to the kind of advantage it gives, and as to the order of precedence between advantage and truth. To put the advantage first, and then to accept such truths as do not interfere with it, is a political proceeding which is favoured far beyond the bounds of what are ordinarily thought of as politics. It is Bagehot's method, and accounts for the relativism which allows him to re-arrange reality incessantly to suit situations, with a foremost eye always on his own. 'Incessant changes in science, in literature, in art, and in politics—in all that forms thinking minds—have made it impossible that really and in fact we should think the same things in 1874 as our ancestors in 1674 or 1774.'[1] Of course: and it is the half truth in this that makes this emphasis acceptable to quick impenetrable minds–even, now that everyone has got used to it, to slow ones. But of course our ancestors are not so unintelligible as all that. The shape of their minds as of their bodies has a distinct resemblance to that of our own, and it is by what used to be regarded as the truth of things that the intelligibility, and the continuity, are possible, just as it is by the truth of things that people together in one place and time can come to an understanding. An absolute relativism is a form of solipsism, which is not the best of bases for the understanding of politics.

This rickety liberalism is nowhere better illustrated than in Bagehot's attack on the Church of England in his article on *The Public Worship Regulation Bill* (1874), which is one of those judgements on current questions in the pages of the *Economist* which Mrs. Barrington admired so much. Needless to say the article is not an overt attack on the Church of England, any more than *The English Constitution* is an overt attack upon the monarchy. It is merely the judicious analysis of a commentator who understands the Church so much better than a convinced Anglican could do. With a sweep of false modesty, Bagehot starts by saying that if the bill 'dealt only with subjects theological or religious', he would not 'interfere in the discussion'. But of course it 'deals also with political questions' on which he did 'not think it right to be silent'.[2] To deprive his judicious readers of his guidance would certainly be very wrong indeed! Without his help they might choose a policy which would produce just the opposite of the effect they intend–a danger against which the *Economist* is still week by week safeguarding its devoted public. There is a characteristic mock deference about this approach to the subject. 'The Church of England is one of those among our institutions which, if it is to be preserved at all'–a point which to any fairminded man must be a matter of serious doubt–'should be

---

[1] *Works*, VI, p. 248.   [2] *ibid.*, p. 247.

touched most anxiously.'[1] When it was last settled, at the Restoration, Locke was still lecturing in Greek and the apple had not fallen on Newton's head. Obviously we could not have much in common with those times. All who understood the growth of banking since 1689 would recognise that religious problems could not be the same then and now. Yet Bagehot in fact ignores the actual differences between 1662 and 1874 and calls the Public Worship Regulation Bill, which was designed to enforce observance of the Prayer Book Rubrics, 'a new Act of Uniformity'.[2] The serious purpose of the several Acts of Uniformity was to preserve the unity of Christians in the places where its writ ran. With this purpose Bagehot's argument has nothing to do; he would have said, no doubt, because he was not dabbling in theology. But in a country in which dissent of every kind– including Papist dissent–had long been allowed to flourish, the purposes of the Act of Uniformity had been abandoned and the basis for the comparison was no longer there. Bagehot is gleeful about the conspicuous way in which the recent history of the English Church had exhibited the native 'indifference to abstract truth'–only it escapes him that abstract truth is, precisely, what Christians are not primarily concerned with. Putting on the guise of a true friend–and how frequently has that been assumed by the worst enemies of the Church?–he argues that 'the real danger of the Establishment is from within, not from without'. Its comprehensiveness was 'a great evil'.[3] Young men of intelligence and education would naturally wish to argue themselves into an extreme position. It irritated Bagehot to see the Establishment look so benignly on differences of opinion. One may say that he had not the imagination to plumb the depths of historic formularies, and his conception of the intelligent young ordinand was of one who showed a similar impatience. 'This is the sort of thought which more and more prevents intellectual young men from taking orders, and we are beginning to see the effect. The moral excellence and the practical piety of the clergy are as good

[1] *ibid.*   [2] *ibid.*, p. 251.   [3] *ibid.*, p. 252.

as ever'–it is the Devil speaking–'but they want individuality of thought and originality of mind.' The ironic praise of political stupidity which appears again and again in Bagehot's work is really the counterpart of an exclusive sympathy with an abstracting cleverness. 'More and more' the clergy 'belong to the most puzzling class to argue with, for more and more they "candidly confess" that they must admit your premises, but "on account of the obscurity of the subject", must decline to draw the inevitable inference.' But is not Trinitarian religion after all a somewhat obscure subject, at any rate for analytical discourse? 'Already this intellectual poorness is beginning to be felt" he goes on, 'and if it should augment, it will destroy the Establishment. She will not have in her ranks arguers who can maintain her position either against those who believe more or against those who believe less.'[1] It is the *pons asinorum* of the rationalist. The 'more' and the 'less' are in themselves a prejudicial definition of the *via media*. The antithesis is a false one for the Anglican who understands the Establishment as merely expressing the political relation of the historic Church in the place he lives in. But Bagehot, like many publicists of enlightenment since his day, sees Romanism on one side and scepticism on the other–either of them a possible position for a rational man–with the derisory Church of England as a refuge for those who are too stupid to adopt a logically coherent position. It should be observed that in this presentation it is not the Roman *Church* which is brought on to the stage but certain Latin habits of mind which show up as clearly in political institutions as in the regulation of ecclesiastical matters. The differences which are being pointed at are those between the Roman law countries and our own.[2] More simply, one may say that, for a common form of imprudent liberalism, any doctrine or institution, however autocratic, which opposes itself to the Establishment, is welcome because it does so oppose itself. Communism as well as Romanism has benefitted by this

[1] *ibid.*, p. 253.
[2] See C. H. Sisson *Spirit of British Administration*, Faber, London, 2nd edition, 1966. *passim*.

indulgence. It is for the disruption they threaten in this country, not for the several orders they would like to establish if they could, that they are admired.

From one point of view Bagehot's liberalism is no more than the voice of commercial enterprise freeing itself from the tyranny of an agricultural system. Commercial enterprise was no novelty of the nineteenth century, but the pace of the industrial revolution and the expansion of credit with which Bagehot was himself concerned had by the mid-century only begun to imagine the possibility of a complete victory. Bagehot always speaks contemptuously of 'these rustics' and resented the social position of the landowning squire, but he was exhilarated by the thought that, on the national stage where bankers and the editor of the *Economist* operated, landowners and the monarchy might be thrown on the rubbish-heap while men of business carried on the affairs of the country. No one could say that this vision of things was belied by the century that followed him. The success of his reading of events is confirmed by the smile on the face of practically every publicist or expert who is allowed to open his mouth in any position from which his voice is likely to be heard. Government is supposed to have become the management of the economy and there is almost universal agreement that it could not be anything else. Impulses of a longer heredity sometimes irrupt upon the scene, but they are the vestiges only of undeveloped minds, as Bagehot believed the monarchy to be.

Yet if there is one lesson of history which is of certain validity it is that a new age is never so new as it imagines. Another is that in this world no one knows very clearly what he is doing until he has done it and it is too late to apply the experience. It is the difficulty of prudence which affords the best argument for reckless exploitation, but in our day the exploiters usually lay claim to a monopoly of prudence as well as of other forms of good sense. There are even those who think that a study of the subordinate prudences of management is a substitute for a humane education. In this shallow world, in which benefits are represented to be as calculable as costs, Bagehot would have been a bounding and no doubt sceptical success. That certainly proves something about his foresight, but unless one holds, as Bagehot himself tended to do, that the contemporary is always right, it proves nothing as to the profundity of his views. Might not Coleridge–the 'dreamy orator', as Bagehot calls him–have been nearer to reality after all? Nothing could be more remote from *The English Constitution* and *Lombard Street* than *Church and State* and *Lay Sermons*. Coleridge's political writings cannot have had a tenth–probably not a twentieth–part of the number of readers Bagehot's have had, and they have had nothing like the same prominence in the minds of politicians, administrators, and the academics of public affairs. What Coleridge wrote, however, can still well up disruptively in the smooth, assured world of those who think like the banker, and they come from a depth and with a force which make Bagehot's little subversions of the Establishment look like a leader in the *Guardian*. It is surprising how much of the ground Bagehot covered is touched on by Coleridge, but in a manner so different that the two sets of writing are less complementary than in hostile tension. It is Bagehot's 'sufferings of the capitalist'[1] against Coleridge's 'when the old labourer's savings, the precious robberies of self-denial from every day's comfort; when the orphan's funds; the widow's livelihood; the fond confiding sister's humble fortune; are found among the victims to the remorseless mania of dishonest speculation, or the desperate cowardice of embarrassment'.[2] Or against this, which might serve as an epigraph to Bagehot's work: 'I cannot persuade myself that the frequency of failures with all the disgraceful secrets of fraud and folly, of unprincipled vanity in expending and desperate speculation in retrieving, can be familiarised to the thoughts and experience of men, as matters of daily occurrence, without serious injury to the moral sense.'[3] Where Bagehot sees the legitimate pursuits of men

[1] *Works*, VII, p. 277.

[2] S. T. Coleridge, *Lay Sermons*, Moxon, London, 3rd edition, 1852, pp. 238-9.

[3] *ibid.*, p. 238

entitled to their complacency Coleridge sees 'the drunken stupor of a usurious selfishness'.[1] No doubt political writings which bristle with allusions to Donne, Jeremy Taylor and Algernon Sydney are barely credible to the readers of the *Economist*, and Coleridge traces the descent of religious thinking from 'that inquisitive and bookish theology'[2] which enabled it to touch the concerns of clever practical men on the raw. No doubt it is true, as he says, that 'formerly men were worse than their principles, but that at present the principles are worse than the men.'[3]

A considerable part of the *Lay Sermons* is devoted to the question, which was ignored by Bagehot and has received little enough attention since, of the balance between agriculture and other pursuits. Coleridge had no idyllic view of the country. He had seen, in what Bagehot calls 'the quiet saving counties', children with their shoulders hunched about their ears, and farmers growing fatter in the very places where the cottagers starved. Nor was he hostile to trade and industry, though he was more interested in the people they produced than in the goods, and could not believe that three people at work in Manchester were necessarily better than two at work in Glencoe or the Trossachs. He was, of course, far from Bagehot's contempt for the ordinary countryman, and he had 'watched many a group of old and young, male and female, going to, or returning from, many a factory'.[4] Although Coleridge passes for being abstracted, and Bagehot for a realist immersed in practical life, it is the latter whose mind rests, in the end, on an abstract calculation and Coleridge who notices what is in front of his nose. In *Church and State*, he attempts to distinguish the respective rôles of agriculture on the one hand and of commerce and industry on the other. He connects the permanence of the state with the land– and is that indeed not a simple matter of fact?–but attributes progression 'in the arts and comforts of life, in the diffusion of the information and knowledge, useful or necessary for all; in

[1] *ibid.*, p. 239.　　　　　[2] *ibid.*, p. 222.
[3] *ibid.*, p. 134.　　　　　[4] *ibid.*, p. 243.

short, all advances in civilization'[1] to the mercantile, manufacturing, distributive and professional classes—a matter of fact
also. But 'agriculture requires principles essentially different from
those of trade; .. a gentleman ought not to regard his estate as a
merchant his cargo, or a shop-keeper his stock'.[2] The continuance
and well-being of those who live on the estate must be a consideration, and 'men . . . ought to be weighed, not counted'.[3] The
objects of the land-owner, with respect to his tenantry and
dependants, are precisely those of the state in relation to the
country as a whole. Both watch over the *dulcia arva* and their
inhabitants. Of course agriculture can be carried on in the spirit
of trade, and this was an aberration which had grown, with ups
and downs, since the establishment of the public debt in the reign
of William III, and had reached what it seemed must be a final
pitch during the Napoleonic Wars, then recently concluded. The
love of lucre was not less in the past, but it met with more and
more powerful checks, among which Coleridge included 'the
ancient feeling of rank and ancestry',[4] the hold and intellectuality
of religion and, following Berkeley, the 'prevailing studies'.[5]
It was against the vestiges of these checks that Bagehot persist-
ently exerted himself, and to what Coleridge called 'a *vortex* of
hopes and hazards, of blinding passions and blind practices',[6]
Bagehot gave another name. The central object of Bagehot's
writing—and it is a destructive one—was to give exclusive respectability to the pursuit of lucre, and to remove whatever social
and intellectual impediments stood in the way of it. Intellectual
pursuits, and whatever strives in the direction of permanence and
stillness, have to give way to the provisional and divisive excite-
ments of gain. In the end one is left contemplating numbers over
a great void.

---

[1] S. T. Coleridge, *On the Constitution of the Church and State according to the Idea of Each*, Pickering, London 1839, p. 26.

[2] S. T. Coleridge, *Lay Sermons*, p. 248.   [3] *ibid.*, p. 243.

[4] *ibid.*, p. 189.   [5] *ibid.*, p. 194.   [6] *ibid.*, p. 235.

It is our own world. Against it, as a better compulsory reading for the young than *Lombard Street*–which however must long have slipped from its position as the one book that all economics students could be counted on to have read–or *The English Constitution*–which is still prominently mentioned–might be set *The Querist*. Bishop Berkeley's questions are too plain and just to excite wide interest, but that should not tell against them. They pose the fundamental questions of economics in relation to government, and these questions ought to be met in a plain form before specious refinements are attempted. *The Querist*'s questions are set in the context of the Ireland of 1735, but they are relevant anywhere precisely because of their appositeness to that country then. The problems were much those that had, in a manner which Bagehot derided, pre-occupied Swift–poverty, luxury, the nature and use of money. He asks:

'5. Whether money be not only so far useful, as it stirreth up industry, enabling men mutually to participate the fruits of each other's labour?

'6. Whether any other means, equally conducing to excite and circulate the industry of mankind, may not be as useful as money?

'7. Whether the real end and aim of men be not power? And whether he who could have everything else at his wish or will would value money? . . .

'Whether human industry can produce, from such cheap materials, a manufacture of so great value by any other art as by those of sculpture and paintings?'(70)[1]

The questions pour out. They are not answered, but they point any unprejudiced enquirer the way to look, and arm him shrewdly to test what is emitted by the plausible expert. Berkeley makes one assumption not shared by Bagehot–the existence of national sovereignty, a notion which did not really interest Bagehot be-cause he saw the body politic, in terms which are extremely pro-vincial in time and place, as a rich cheese in which men of

[1] *The Works of George Berkeley Bishop of Cloyne*, edited by A. A. Luce and T. E. Jessop, Nelson, London, 1948–57, Vol. VI, pp. 105–11.

business could wriggle in their financial contortions undisturbed.
'20. If power followeth money, whether this can be anywhere
more properly and securely placed, than in the same hands
wherein the supreme power is already placed?
'83. But whether a bank that utters bills, with the sole view of
promoting the public weal, may not so proportion their quantity
as to avoid several inconveniences which might attend private
banks?'[1]

Secrecy in financial transactions, the opportunities for private
profit-making at the expense of the public good or out of private
trust—the rights which Bagehot held most dear—are to Berkeley
so many cankers to be cut out where that is possible. What makes
him so disarming is the perfect balance of his mind. The man who
was dazzled by the visible universe had an equal charity like
Traherne's. He is genuinely disinterested, and cares more for
his country than for himself. It must pass for a strange abnormality
beside the extreme normality, not to say commonplaceness, of
Bagehot's busy self-preservation. Thought turns in the end on
what lies at the bottom of the mind. One scarcely likes, for shame,
to quote Berkeley's *Maxims concerning Patriotism*,[2] but they are all
true.

The basis of Berkeley's economics is no doubt a version of that
mercantilism which was condemned by Adam Smith and which
for Bagehot, in the euphoria of his enlightenment, was no longer
more than a figment in an age which understood the true way of
making money. But something of that kind is unkillable as long
as the notion of sovereignty and of the *aris et focis* is not killed.
Adam Smith on Mercantilism is like a reader of the *Daily Tele-
graph* on the evils of socialism, though it would greatly surprise
most of those readers to learn that the exercise of a strong arm on
industry and commerce was not an invention of Karl Marx.
Berkeley's interventionism springs from his care for the people
starving among the green acres of Ireland:
'173. Whether the quantities of beef, butter, wool and leather,

---

[1] *ibid.*, pp. 170, 174.   [2] *ibid.*, p. 253ff.

exported from this island, can be reckoned the superfluities of a country, where there are so many natives naked and famished?'[1]

One might say that Berkeley recommends prudence as to the public interest, and a certain recklessness as to private interest, while Bagehot's recklessness is for the public, and his caution is for himself.

What we get from Bagehot is not so much a theory as a position, and not so much a position as a form of tactics. It is Walter Bagehot whom the successive positions are intended to protect— the Walter Bagehot who slipped down the crack between Unitarianism and Anglicanism; who was the child of the Bank House as some are sons of the manse; whose money was better than that of the squire's but did not produce better effects on the locals; who should have been educated at Oxford but was above that sort of conformism; who conformed instead to the world of business but was cleverer than its other inhabitants; who was all the time worried about the sanity of his stock and did not have any children; who distrusted the hereditary powers and owed all his opportunities to family influence. He was a gifted man who pushed around in the world, and he liked to think that there was only pushing and shoving, though he owed more to the discretion which keeps people on the winning side. No doubt a great deal of life is like this, and more than any other writer of talent Bagehot embodies the forces of successful action. But it is successful action in a particular *milieu*, that of the rising finance and journalism of nineteenth-century England. Bagehot operated in a field of natural selection from which the more desperate assaults, and the more desperate risks, had already been eliminated. Put him beside Raleigh, and one misses the moral strength which comes of a readiness to contemplate stabbing, and of the necessity in certain circumstances of facing the block. Put him beside

---

[1] *ibid.*, p. 119.

Swift, one misses the force of instinctive but intellectually developed loyalties. The comparisons are in a sense unfair, because Bagehot could be–and was–a man of ability without being able to hold a candle to either of the other two; but they serve to designate not only his stature but his kind. And Bagehot was not always successful, even in his world of limited practice. The election at Bridgwater shows a certain gaucherie. It suggests also that Bagehot was a man who receded from his failures rather than lived through them. Perhaps the current of petty affairs carried him too strongly. Swift the Dean of Saint Patrick's knew that he had not been as much in Harley's confidence as he had supposed, when he lived in the great world, and his real success was made out of his defeat. Raleigh drank from the bottom of the well before he had finished. Bagehot does not, in his writing, anywhere touch these profounder depths. He spins clever comment between himself and reality; he has skimmed the river not dredged it.

Yet one should not under-rate the peculiarity of Bagehot's performance. Although by definition there are common men enough, who do the ordinary business of the world and avoid doing it on any particular principle, it is rare indeed for such a man to be explicit about this performance. Even Bagehot hedges a little, but the more one reads him the more it strikes one how little it is. The references to religion are modified by a social tone; he is a man accustomed to not offending the ladies. But the irony and contempt show through. Bagehot is reluctant to abandon the ordinary direction of his vision, which is downwards, with an amused smile playing on his lips. 'Your governess is like an egg', he said to the Miss Wilsons when he first met them, and as soon as the unfortunate hireling's back was turned. The Miss Wilsons tittered. How clever Mr. Bagehot was so to break in on the traditional respects. The little episode is perfectly in the tone of Bagehot's political writings. It is a tone which has for a century been sure of a certain applause, but it indicates limitations in the speaker as well as in any audience that is too readily amused by it. It excludes any sympathy which threatens the desiderated victory.

It is quite different from the tone of Samuel Johnson, when he talked for victory, for Johnson cared for the truth more than for himself and the victory was mere knock-about stuff. His real purpose was to remove his opponent's pretensions till the vanquished like the victor was humbled before reality. Bagehot's anxiety is to get by, and never to admit that he has come to grief, which is, truly, the tone of affairs and the reason why they so rarely comport the seriousness of the confrontations which are habitual in the artist or other penitent.

However well Bagehot's tactics conform to the practice of everyday life, they lack the substance of a political or social theory because, with all the pretence of frankness there is an unwillingness to admit that they are viable only within a certain defence line. Bagehot's blasphemy is that of a man who feels himself to be securely protected from God. His financial confidence tricks are played out in a society which permits and encourages certain forms of depredation. He can laugh at what he pretends are the powers that be simply because the powers are in reality not there, or because he does not tax them in any way to which they would really object, however rude they might think him. A man who is really inside the spirit of his age, as Bagehot was, cannot really offend important people, because they are working within the same pre-suppositions as himself. The most he can do is to get the credit for being a little advanced. This is the very type of the liberalism which grew up within the frontiers of the England who was a terror to her foes or, at the very least, could make them think twice. Liberalism does not flourish except within safe frontiers and that is, of course, one of the reasons for making the frontiers safe, so long as that is practicable. So long as there are life-and-death confrontations within a country, there are other pre-occupations than liberalism. It was not in evidence when Cranmer was burnt or when Laud was beheaded. It reached an intense florescence under the roof of King's College, Cambridge, in the twentieth century, when personal relations, without even the degree of natural realism which is imported by the phenomena of hetero-sexuality, were amusingly believed to hold a real primacy over the prejudices not only of religion but of patriotism. There is a classic statement in E. M. Forster's *What I Believe*, printed as a pamphlet in 1939 and reproduced in *Two Cheers* (just the number to bring an understanding smile) *for Democracy* (1951). Forster of course did not believe in belief, and that was the first irony of his pamphlet. One simply had to have a creed because all the rough chaps outside Abinger and King's insisted on having one. 'Tolerance, good temper and sympathy are no longer enough in a world which is rent by religious and racial persecution, in a world where ignorance rules, and science, who ought to have ruled, plays the subservient pimp.'[1] By implication, it is in a world just recently invented that tolerance, good temper and sympathy are not enough—as if those qualities had ever brought home the bacon, or defined the nature of man, however desirable they might be as supervening graces. 'Science ought to have ruled'. But whatever that evocative phrase may mean—and it would certainly have been good for *three* cheers in Cambridge— the idea that there is any novelty about ignorance being on top is a new one indeed. It was just 'for the moment',[2] according to Forster, that his favourite virtues wanted stiffening, simply as a necessary antidote to the men in jack-boots. Forster has the vulgarity to produce as his 'motto' an inversion of certain words recorded in St. Mark as having been spoken to our Lord. He makes out—for in 1939 a touch of social deference was still thought prudent, as regards Jesus himself—that his opponents are simply Moses and Paul—as if that might not in itself have given him pause. But according to Mark, Jesus said: 'If thou canst believe, all things are possible to him that believeth. And straight- way the father of the child cried out, and said with tears, Lord, I believe; help thou mine unbelief.'[3] Forster's silly motto was 'Lord, I disbelieve—help thou my unbelief.'[4] He illustrates his folly by putting the shallow Erasmus side by side with the profoundly sceptical Montaigne.

---

[1] E. M. Forster, *Two Cheers for Democracy*, Arnold, London, 1951, p. 77.
[2] *ibid.*   [3] Mark 9, v. 23–4.   [4] E. M. Forster, *op. cit.*, p. 77.

Forster's *credo*, like Bagehot's, is an amused disowning of everything which is not himself. In place of the banker-journalist— a crude, masculine figure in comparison—is the troop of 'the sensitive, the considerate and the plucky'.[1] Readers of the novels will know who is meant—the cosy snobs of *Howard's End*, the picnickers of *A Passage to India*, no one far away from the Abinger-Cambridge axis, for the attempts to get beyond this special *milieu*, in such a person as Leonard Bast, for example, serve only to show Forster's real incomprehension of the human animal. For in all he says it is an ambience, not the person, that counts. Indeed in Cambridge it apparently took Psychology (sic) to show 'that there is something incalculable in each of us, which may at any moment rise to the surface and destroy our normal balance'.[2] My word! No one would have guessed that before Psychology. To Forster's special group of 'the sensitive, the considerate and the plucky' are attributed all the culture-objects Forster approves of. These people 'produce literature and art, or they do disinterested scientific research', they 'are creative in their private lives'. They even 'found religions',[3] which you might have thought, on Forster's principles, was not a very good thing to do, but it is important that all creativity should belong to the gang. This is Forster's version of the *élite* which is author-ised to be superior about the body politic, as Bagehot's is the free-masonry of *Economist* readers. Man for man, one might as well have Bagehot's lot. Bagehot is anyway more honest as to what he is about. The culture gang is perhaps naturally more aberrational. Anyhow Forster's aberration extends to claiming Dante as belonging to his set, on the ground that he placed Brutus and Cassius in the lowest circle of Hell 'because they had chosen to betray their friend Julius Caesar rather than their country Rome',[4] though in fact they were put there because they had betrayed their *master*, the type in that circle being Judas Iscariot.

The protected world of E. M. Forster is really a pleasure-garden, for those who care for that sort of pleasure and can

---

[1] *ibid.*, p. 82.   [2] *ibid.*, p. 77.   [3] *ibid.*, p. 79.   [4] *ibid.*, p. 78.

afford high walls to live behind. Forster's admiration for his own irradiation and that of his friends knew no bounds. With mock humility and a blasphemous allusion he says: 'And one can, at all events, show one's own little light here, one's own poor little trembling flame, with the knowledge that it is not the only light that is shining in the darkness, and not the only one which the darkness does not comprehend.'[1] From behind the high walls where the plucky and the sensitive have taken refuge come sniggers at the ordinary affairs of men and the great historical movements. It is a mark not merely of irreligion but of lack of grasp of the concerns of mankind that Forster refers to the Christian Church as 'a worthy stunt'[2] – like a flag-day, no doubt, or one of those petitions to which he was a never-failing sub-scriber. That these frolics were conditional Forster himself perfectly understood. 'While we are trying to be sensitive and ad-vanced and affectionate and tolerant' – I am not at all sure that such *effort* is to be commended, but that is what Forster says – 'an unpleasant question pops up: does not all society rest upon force?' His theory was that 'all the great creative actions, all the decent human relations, occur during the intervals when force has not managed to come to the front'.[3] The crucifixion, for example? It is this notion of 'the intervals that matter' which makes Forster's lib-eralism so fragile and artificial. He confesses to 'looking the other way' until fate strikes him, and one can admire the candour of that, if nothing else. But the corporate affairs of men are not so to be understood. The roots of trouble are always there, even in our most smiling actions. King's and Abinger are not cases of virtue, but the slight phenomena of an historical situation which for a brief space allows a few rather soft people so to amuse themselves, and to con-sume what others have sweated or got themselves killed for. Perhaps the esthete, like the banker, depends on 'the ruder sort of men' who 'will sacrifice all they hope for, *themselves*, for what is called an idea'.[4]

A more important question is whether theories of liberalism, whether economic or otherwise intellectual, which can have play

---

[1] *ibid.*   [2] *ibid.*, p. 83.   [3] *ibid.*, p. 80.   [4] v. *supra*, p. 67.

only because of the antecedence of less seductive institutions and doctrines, can be more than a delusive foundation for political thought. So long as they are understood to be merely a conditional arrangement, a permitted sport within a certain constitutional framework, they may have their usefulness, for they certainly embody a part of civilisation. It is in their nature, however, to nibble at the framework rather than to support it. That again may have its uses, for all institutions must change and be ceaselessly in a state of adaptation. The 'hard facts' of money are not very hard, for they are the facts of a convention, and the 'values' of intellectual fashion are valuable only so far as they represent a viable existence.

The enlightenment Bagehot offered has run out. A good laugh at the monarchy, a series of little jeers at the historical Church, a jealous look at the gentry–all this comported a certain amusement in its time, but it is not very funny now. The gentry has gone the way it has always gone, in England where, as Fuller said in 1648, the capacity to be gentle has not been denied to any, who so behaves himself. The 'Church is more set against the world than at any time since pagan Rome',[1] as Eliot had it. No one can deny now that she is engaged in a life-and-death struggle, which is all she is fit for. The monarchy has gone on, not, as Bagehot suggested, because people at large have not noticed that the Cabinet really takes the decisions, but because they have begun to suspect that the Cabinet does not either. The final point in the State must rest on a certain incomprehension, and incomprehension is the beginning of theology. Few people now would imagine that they knew what was meant by the Divine Right of Kings, but anyone might reach the point of mystification

---

[1] T. S. Eliot, 'Thoughts after Lambeth', in *Selected Essays*, Faber, London 1932, p. 363.

as to the coherence and persistence of national entities, which the hereditary monarchy so well expresses.

Gregory Dix reports that he met in West Africa, 'a leading Ju-Ju man' who explained his rôle as a magician with 'all the *aplomb* and that touch of courteous condescension which always mark the man of science explaining to the theologian'.[1] The witch-doctor claimed to make spectacular things happen, and thought the priest was wasting his time. It was, of course, the former who was the typical man of the modern world. Nobody now likes to admit to being lacking in usefulness, of some kind intelligible to a vulgar utilitarianism. Yet the production of results is a less common achievement than most performers would have us believe. There is still hewing of wood and drawing of water, but such clear cases are by no means universal in an industrial society. When one gets to the men with charts and statistics–the battalions of management so characteristic of our world, whose philosophy is exclusively one of *results*–the connection between cause and effect is often so tenuous as to strain everyone's belief. The idea that a man 'makes' even money, as distinct from putting himself or perhaps merely standing in the way of it, is always to be treated with reserve. And even with the housewife, that residual handiwoman from earlier times, the rôle is a much larger thing than the sum of the performances. In a static, caste society, it is the rôle which dominates and attracts attention. The warrior occasionally fights, but is always a warrior. In our sort of society, it is conceived that the worth of a man is in the result he produces, so there is no end to this sort of exaggeration. Yet results, even when achieved, are generally very difficult to evaluate, and the idea of a whole society valuing itself on its results alone is a very difficult conception indeed. One might say indeed that it is nonsense. A simple deception has given it currency–the peculiar, not to say overwhelming, use of money in our times. A conventional numerical system establishes a common

---

[1] Gregory Dix, *Jew and Greek, A Study in the Primitive Church*, Dacre Press, London, 1953, p. 93.

value, and it is pretended that one can calculate a Gross National Product, within which all results have their contributory number.

Bagehot was entirely a man of this world. His personal product was only words and numbers – the typical groceries of managerial man – but he was the philosopher of the consumer society, which is only the reverse of the producer obverse. The end of progress was 'the development of human comfort',[1] then the distinguishing mark of the superiority of the Englishman. Bagehot saw this as the product of industry by the development of money-lending, and this corresponds pretty well to an obvious aspect of history in the hundred years since his death. It was a sort of liberation, involving the denigration of everything which stood in the way of it, but the liberation is hardly what we notice most about the world it has brought about.

Bagehot was reckless even on his own showing. He saw that there had to be recognised authority to hold any society together, and that the establishment of authority was a process which takes time, a lot of time.[2] It was a sort of non-financial capital, he might have said, which could be used only when it had been collected or imagined. He was interested in the *use* – what could be done, in his case money-making – under its shadow. None the less the whole tenor of his critical effort was to assist the destruction of respect among those whom he regarded as serious and intelligent men of affairs, for what he called the dignified elements of the constitution. It was as if to ensure that no future generation should operate with such advantages. Perhaps he did not care much for the future. The old landowner planted trees for his grandchildren; the man acting in the spirit of trade wants to know only how much timber he can sell over the next five years. Coleridge's distinction goes to the root of the matter. Any political unit worth maintaining, or which is anyway to be maintained at all, must contain a principle of foresight and continuity which goes beyond the next series of trade figures, and it will be the foresight of care rather than of calculation. An unreasoning love

[1] v. *supra*, p. (136).   [2] v. *supra*, p. (98).

on the part of its inhabitants is the best safeguard for any country—superior even to that love of private gain in which Adam Smith and Bagehot, like Mandeville before them, put such trust. No doubt both stimuli are necessary, the world being what it is, but it is superstition, or worse, to suppose that the unchecked appetite for lucre can bring anything but the destruction of the commonwealth, or that it can take very long to produce that result. Art and all things made for their own sake tell in the other direction, towards permanence rather than towards change and saleability, and there is no more terrifying symptom of decay than the replacement of art, in the public attention, by the saleable products of anti-art. Those who do not believe that that is happening do not know what art is. They can never have *seen* the ordinary domestic equipment of the seventeenth century, or tradesmen's cards of the eighteenth century. The Devil has many disguises, and what is called liberty of expression, particularly in the great trade of sex, has more to do with the nature of the financial system than with art. In the ordinary hue and cry about the latest play or novel to poke its way to prominence, it is more instructive to ask who gets the money from it than whether the work can properly be regarded as corrupting. Indeed the financial question has more to do with serious literary criticism. It must not even be supposed that there is some special kinship between art and democracy. Indeed almost all of the great literature of the world was produced without that freedom of expression which is now generally said to be essential for such productions.

It will not quite do, in a commonwealth, to count heads as one counts money. The land is also important. It was until recently maintained that there was a labour shortage in this country. Nothing could be more absurd, in an island of this size. It was merely that people were doing the wrong things, because the wrong things were the most profitable. It is now often maintained that if we make and sell enough of any kind of marketable rubbish, our future is assured. That also is a lie. An economics which rests entirely on financial measurement is as far from reality as any refinement of mediaeval schoolmen. It will not help if there is nothing to eat in the refrigerator, or the land is soured from Portsmouth to the Wash.

Bagehot lies under an ungainly tombstone in the churchyard of All Saints, Langport, which looks out over miles of Somerset to the Dorset hills. Standing there one may see why he was, indeed, no more than 'the wisest man of his generation'.

EPILOGUE

There is, of course, another view of Walter Bagehot. This is
that he was the innovator who pointed the way for all reasonable
Anglo-Saxons in the generations which have succeeded him. It
is possible to see him as pointing further than that, as if the
give-away attitude he represents – giving away what belongs to
others while holding tight to what you have yourself – were the
only rational way of conducting affairs, in all times and even in
those places which have not been illuminated by the light of Anglo-
Saxondom. In a way it is, if by rational you mean proceeding
so far as possible to a comfortable disintegration. Only you
have to be sure that you have something to give you comfort
as long as you need it. Not everyone has been so well placed
in that respect, as the English middle classes of the nineteenth
or even the twentieth century. The case for attributing a wider
relevance to this attitude is confidence in the power of technology
to create, continuously, more than we manage to destroy.
This confidence is inherent in all the dominant movements of
our world and one can entertain the hypothesis that it may be
justified.

In Bagehot's time things must have looked rather different.
But the direction of movement was already marked, and the year
in which Bagehot was educated by the French *coup d'état* was also
the year of the Great Exhibition. It is therefore possible to hold
that the adolescent who, nine years before (in 1842) had entered
upon courses of study at University College, London, rather than
go to Oxford, had been guided by all the lights of advancing
thought. The same planets which presided over Walter Bagehot's
birth had played upon the seven acres around Gower Street which

ere purchased in 1826 and where the foundation stone of the
College was laid in the following year. Behind the founding
movement were impeccable Whig minds. There was Brougham,
of whom Bagehot himself said that he 'was able to rush hither
and thither . . . and gather up the whole stock of the most recent
information, the extreme decimals of the statistics, and diffuse
them immediately with eager comment to a listening world.'[1]
There was Thomas Campbell, an overblown literary man whose
best work was behind him and who was busying himself with a
career of public eminence. Both were Scots, educated at Scotch
universities, and fell easily into the tradition of those who, since
the Act of Union to which Swift had taken such exception, had
contributed to the inflation of the English and Anglican world
and its replacement by Great Britain or something even greater
and vaguer. Other members of the founding group were Isaac
Lyon Goldsmid, Joseph Hume, and 'some influential dissenters,
most of them connected with the congregation of Dr. Cox of
Hackney'. The scheme was inspired by the same passion for
freedom which motivated Thomas Bagehot—an aversion from
the Thirty-Nine Articles with which Oxford and Cambridge were
so degradingly entangled. The first Council of the new institution
comprised representatives of nearly every religious denomination,
and so demonstrated the unimportance of such differences and
ultimately that of the Christian religion itself. The ideas of the
reformers were much the same as those which Sir William
Hamilton—another Scot—brought into play in the eighteen-
thirties against the sleepy resistance of Oxford. Hamilton's aim
was to lower the pride of the fellows and to raise that of the
professors, as the supposed sources of learning in particular subjects. From the first it was planned that the courses of instruction
in London should include languages, mathematics, physics, the
mental and moral sciences, the laws of England, history and
political economy. These developments must have been noted
with satisfaction in the office of the bank manager at Langport,

---

[1] *Works*, II, p. 302; E. III, 159.

and no doubt Thomas Bagehot recoiled with horror at the reaction which led in 1831 to the opening of King's College, London. At King's a similar pattern of studies was to be followed but there was to be a connection with the national church. The sentiment of Thomas Bagehot would have been those of the contemporary cartoonist who exhibited three fat bishops huzza-ing for King's set in a scale against Brougham, Campbell and Jeremy Bentham. The bishops bore down the scale—as if they were not fat enough already—with a weight labelled 'Money and Interest', while the reformers of University College flew up in the air, having nothing on their side but 'Sense and Science'.

There is no doubt that, in accordance with a well-known bit of social mechanics, the activities of the dissenting groups had a marked effect in stimulating, somewhat belatedly, the forces of orthodoxy. The foundation of the University of Durham from the revenues of that see may be classed as an effect of the same movement. It was to the rising forces of dissent and industry that the Bagehot family really belonged. One must not over-rate the intellectual freshness of those forces or the degree of social oppression they suffered. They followed the Whigs who, throughout most of the eighteenth century, had treated the Church with contempt while ensuring that their nominees revelled in the revenues of the bishoprics. The alliance with industry which was characteristic of the nineteenth century was in succession to a long alliance with the forces of finance. When Matthew Arnold took up the task of civilising dissent, from the point of view of an Oxford which by then he regarded as a home of lost causes, it was the manufacturers and their opinionated chapels he had in mind. Arnold was, rather markedly, the son of a public school head-master—*the* public school headmaster, you might say—and himself an inspector of schools. But his class of savage mill-owners themselves begat inspectors of schools and the like in great numbers and it was finally the war of 1914–18 which split society open and made it clear that the landed aristocracy and gentry whose dignity had offended Bagehot so much, would offend by their dignity no more. Dissent, in a wider sense than the *démo-*

business of disagreement with the Thirty-Nine Articles, became the unquestionable Establishment of our society. It has been so, with an ever-widening series of topics if a certain monotony of method, ever since.

There is an intellectual succession to be taken account of in this movement away from what one might perhaps call the agricultural and religious world to the modern world of assumptions about the impugnability of technological benefits–a tradition of feeling, as Keynes has pointed out, as well as of thought. It is– to quote Keynes's essay on Malthus, 'the English tradition of humane science . . . that tradition of Scotch and English thought, in which there has been, I think, an extraordinary continuity of *feeling*, if I may so express it, from the eighteenth century to the present time–the tradition which is suggested by the names of Locke, Hume, Adam Smith, Paley, Bentham, Darwin and Mill, a tradition marked by a love of truth and a most noble lucidity, by a prosaic sanity free from sentiment or metaphysic, and by an immense disinterestedness and public spirit.'[1] It is to this tradition, or only a little aside from it–aside on account of his personal flavour and the tinge which financial interests gave to his concern for the public good–that Bagehot belongs, as does Keynes himself, though with another, and perhaps subtler, deviation. For Keynes was, in his early years, at the centre of a little pseudo-renaissance which was a great social and, it is said, literary and intellectual success. This movement marks the passing of the non-conformist tradition into the general orthodoxy of Bloomsbury and the *New Statesman* and beyond. Keynes has given a nostalgic account of this in the short paper, entitled *My Early Beliefs*, which he wrote in September, 1938, just as it became publicly indisputable that the smile of amusement which had, so to speak, passed with an immense accretion of refinement from Bagehot to himself, was not, after all, a smile at the nature of reality but the tic of a rather pampered group. Keynes was of course among the first to see this for he had, like Bagehot, a

[1] J. M. Keynes, *Essays in Biography*, Macmillan, London, 1933, p. 120.

facility in withdrawing from untenable positions, though in this personal confession his subtlety in preserving his own dignity was such that, while admitting that he had been wrong, he added that it was too late to change. There had, after all, been only 'just a grain of truth' in D. H. Lawrence's assertion, in 1914, that Keynes and his Cambridge friends were 'done for', and it was only by ignoring what Keynes called 'our charm, our intelligence, our unworldliness, our affection,' that the admission could be forced thus far. The centre of their doctrine, or 'religion' as Keynes appropriately called it, was an individualism which was not, like Bagehot's, that of a moneyed provincial pushing his way in a conventional society, but that of a man who felt himself safely detached from all such ugly realities.

'We entirely repudiated', Keynes says, 'a personal liability on us to obey general rules. We claimed the right to judge every individual case on its merits, and the wisdom, experience and self-control to do so successfully. This was a very important part of our faith, violently and aggressively held, and for the outer world it was our most obvious and dangerous characteristic. We repudiated entirely customary morals, conventions and traditional wisdom. We were, that is to say, in the strict sense of the term, immoralists. The consequences of being found out had, of course, to be considered for what they were worth. But we recognised no moral obligation on us, no inner sanction, to conform or to obey. Before heaven we claimed to be our own judge in our own case. I have come to think that this is, perhaps, rather a Russian characteristic. It is certainly not an English one.' And yet it is, of course, the logical outcome of that long line of dissent which, having eluded all the authorities which it always asserted were bent on oppressing it, ends by being dissent *tout court*, or the mere pursuit of a lonely appetite. Keynes goes on: 'It resulted in a general, widespread, though partly covert, suspicion affecting ourselves, our motives and our behaviour. This suspicion still persists to a certain extent, and it always will. It has deeply coloured the course of our lives in relation to the outside world. It is, I now think, a justifiable suspicion. Yet so far as I am concerned, it is too late to change. I remain, and always will remain, an immoralist.'[1]

Certainly Keynes had gone beyond Bagehot in the logic of his argument. He kept better logical company, and had less to fear from society than Bagehot, whose credit depended on retaining, in spite of his cleverness, a certain stodgy respectability, while Keynes was throughout his life able to cultivate a reputation as an intellectual. He was moving towards a world in which a much more rapid adaptability was required and Bagehot's gentle jeering at the Church and the landed gentry was old-fashioned stuff. Keynes's beliefs left no impediment to limitless change, and this enabled him to carry much further the sort of rationality which is needed for the uninhibited development of technology. He thought, as Bagehot did, that 'self-interest was *rational*' and that 'the egoistic and altruistic systems' would 'work out in practice to the same conclusions.'[2] This optimistic view of human nature he claimed later to have corrected, though not, I think, so far as to take a pessimistic view of himself and his friends, whom he called, in a Forsterian phrase, 'poor, silly, well-meaning us'.[3] Bagehot of course always made a point of the stupidity of other people, or of the mass which needed to have deceptions practised upon it so that those who could see through social and religious pretences could govern the country.

Keynes was perhaps the wisest man of *his* generation, as Bagehot was of his, and that is after all the height of wordly distinction. An hereditary member of the post-clerical university world, he was born at the right moment to rise with its fortunes as an influence on public policy. He had all the talents for a distinguished rôle. Eton and King's College, Cambridge, gave him a background which facilitated his access to political circles at a time when they were only just beginning to lose their aristocratic or at any rate upper class colour. He was present at the Peace negotiations in 1919. After a recession from favour said to have

---

[1] J. M. Keynes, *Two Memoirs*, London, Rupert Hart-Davis, 1949, pp. 97–8.
[2] *ibid.*, p. 99.   [3] *ibid.*, p. 103.

been due to *The Economic Consequences of the Peace*, a book which was in the rising sentiment of the inter-war years, whatever might be thought of its political acuteness, he was back at the centre of power in the Second War and afterwards, with a theory which fitted perfectly the social-democratic tendencies of the time. He was the prophet, only shortly before politicians were ready to receive the doctrine, of central controls which would establish 'an aggregate volume of output corresponding to full employment as nearly as is practicable', and consequentially of 'a large extension of the traditional functions of government'.[1] The *direction* of output was all right; whatever was produced, was good. It was only the volume–the fact that it left people unemployed–that was wrong.

Economics used to be called Political Economy, and has lost the adjective in the search for scientific status. But political it remains, like the behavioural sciences at large, which are sciences only in a large, old-fashioned sense, whatever may be the claims of their academic exponents, scrambling for the most profitable description in order to get a full share of the money flowing into universities. Concealed under the more comprehensive propositions of these sciences, and under all their practical propositions, are assumptions about the nature of the human animal which are capable of only slight modification in the light of current observations and are mainly lore–what the human race thinks about itself. Keynes was well aware of the underlying elusiveness of his subject-matter. In propounding his *General Theory of Employment* he realised that it was uncertain 'how far it is safe to stimulate the average propensity to consume' and that only experience would show 'how far the common will, embodied in the policy of the state, ought to be directed to increasing and supplementing the inducement to invest.'[2] The 'common will', so unobtrusively introduced, begs all the classic questions of political theory. It could only get by because of the general agreement not

[1] J. M. Keynes: *The General Theory of Employment, Interest and Money*, London, Macmillan, 1936, pp. 378–9.

[2] *ibid.*, p. 377.

to question the bases of democracy. Keynes the theorist was always near enough to practice to know when to keep his mouth shut. Bagehot's conception of a managing *élite* was franker but it flattered the degree of democracy obtaining in his day. In Keynes's day the public to be flattered was larger. Enough attention has not been given to the effect of the extension of the franchise upon economic theory. Bagehot wanted to stop the tide of widening suffrage at a point convenient to him, beyond which it would have spoiled his theories and perhaps his income. Keynes did not sufficiently take account of its effects, though he clearly realised that his projects could only be executed by the intervention of the state. What sort of state? and What was it likely to do? were questions he brought his theory up against but did not, in the end, face. Both he and Bagehot assumed the sort of state they respectively needed. It is a measure of the benign good fortune of their lives, and a limitation in their usefulness to us.

Keynes concluded his *General Theory* with some words which look far beyond the subject-matter, beyond economics altogether. 'The ideas of economists and political philosophers,' he says, 'both when they are right and when they are wrong, are more powerful than is commonly understood. Indeed the world is ruled by little else. Practical men, who believe themselves to be quite exempt from any intellectual influences, are usually the slave of some defunct economist.'[1] He might have added that economists and political philosophers, in the most enlightened epochs as in the darkness of the Victorian Age or of the Middle Ages, take their direction from religious and ethical conceptions which they are apt to think they threw out of their studies when they started their serious work. Ideas are not created by individuals; they are derived.

In our day the denial of the sources of our thinking is an indispensable preliminary to any intervention on the public stage. Debate on public affairs, and still more the actual execution of public business, has to be conducted on the basis that there are

[1] *ibid.*, p. 383.

facts but no philosophies. It is a technique for securing civil peace and in view of the difficulty, historically speaking, of attaining this objective, it is not to be lightly dismissed. Whereas, however, older Machiavellian devices for achieving one's ends amidst general approval–such as, in suitable times and places, assuming a mask of religion–allow for a realistic disjunction between the thought of the governor and of the governed, this device is apt to deceive the governors as well. The modern bureaucratic machine, certainly in this country, is conducted in the full belief–tempered only by the private scepticism of individual operators–in the objectivity of 'facts'. It needs a poet rather than a mathematician to realise vividly the shadowy and elusive connection between word and fact.

Bagehot was a founding father of the apologetics of 'fact.' Clever, sceptical men of affairs, the class whose activity consisted in deceiving the others, saw, according to him, nothing else, and what the others saw was nothing. Facts were what Bagehot could use, to clear a way for himself in society and to make money. They are likewise the weapon of the contemporary civil servant, to turn away wrath and to make a game so complicated that no one else can play it.

The function of the philosopher, the artist, or in his degree of any man worth his salt, is different. Wyndham Lewis said despairingly: 'The game of government goes on, and it is a game that no philosopher has ever been able to interrupt seriously for a moment.'[1] Bagehot on the other hand tried to elevate to the rôle of a philosophy the derivative muddlings of men of affairs, to the detriment of both theory and practice.

[1] v. C. H. Sisson: *The Politics of Wyndham Lewis*, in *Agenda*, Wyndham Lewis Special Issue, Autumn-Winter 1969–70.

INDEX